Florian Neumann
The 'Spirit' of Self-Sacrifice
PART ONE

The 'Spirit' of Self-Sacrifice

Hiraizumi Kiyoshi (1895-1984) and the Perception of History in Imperial Japan

Florian Neumann

PART ONE

Up to the Eve of Pearl Harbor

Content

Introduction   I

1. Fukui-Echizen and the 'Kenmu Restoration'   II
    1. 1. Studying History at Tōkyō Imperial University   23
    1. 2. Embracing the 'Japanese Spirit'   26
    1. 3. Being abroad in Europe, 1930-1931   33

2. 'Times of National Emergency', the 1930s   37
    2. 1. Gaining public weight   43
    2. 2. The Kenmu Restoration's 600th anniversary   50
    2. 3. 'The February 26 Incident'   58

3. The Road into War, 1937-1941   63
    3. 1. Professorships for the History of Japanese Thought   68
    3. 2. Expanding on the Philosophy of Death   72
    3. 3. Konoe's 'New Order', 1940   78

Notes   88
Glossary   109
Bibliography   120

Hiraizumi Kiyoshi

Introduction

With the 'Meiji Restoration' (*Meiji ishin*) in 1868 Japan entered into the phase of quickly becoming a modern nation after being ruled for more than 250 years by a feudal system under the Tokugawa Shogunate (1600-1868). But as the country rapidly—and hastily—began modernizing under the slogan of 'Civilization and Enlightenment' (*bunmei kaika*), a coalition faction around the nativist *kokugaku* ('National Learning') movement, that since the eighteenth century had advocated a 'return to the ancient way' (*fukko*) of an imagined state of the past, sought to establish a fundamentalist system based on their Shintō beliefs in which Japan had been created by the mythical Emperor Jinmu in 660 BC according to the two historical tales from the eighth century, the *Kojiki* (»Records of Ancient Matters«) and the *Nihon shoki* (»The Chronicles of Japan«). These advocates of a verbatim 'Restoration' were swiftly sidelined from power in 1869. The scholar Marius B. Jansen explained how the Meiji oligarchy, "intent on building a state capable of holding its own in the modern world, bent Shinto to their purposes without allowing it to distract them from the work at hand."[1] He further stated:

> *In practice … the attempt to restore the institutions of antiquity in their entirety and to adopt Shinto theocracy once more was soon rejected by the Meiji leaders. Antiquity could be invoked and put aside. But not entirely, and not at all where the imperial institution was concerned. The ritual and aura of a vanished past was put to work in the task of modernizing the country, as when the promulgation of the Charter Oath in April 1868 was surrounded with the panoply of the past.*

This initial attempt to recreate the ideal state of antiquity was underlined by an 'Imperial Rescript for the Study of History' (*shūshi no shō*) in April 1869 that announced the creation of an 'Office for Historiography' (*shikyoku*) to reinstate the task of compiling an authoritative historical account under the Emperor's tutelage, which had been abandoned after the *'Six National Histories'* (*rikkokushi*) of the Nara (710-794) and Heian (794-1185) periods, when the Throne in Kyōto lost its political power to the Kamakura Shogunate (1185-1333). As Margaret Mehl wrote, "following the Chinese tradition of dynastic histories, the compilation of a definite standard history (*seishi*) came to be regarded as the task of a legitimate government, and in early Meiji the *seishi* remained the ideal of historiography, just as the imperial bureaucratic state was a political ideal."[3] The edict read:

> *Historiography is a forever eternal state ritual* (taiten) *and a superb act of Our Ancestors. But after the Six National Histories it was interrupted and no longer continued. What a huge deficiency! Now the evil of misrule by the warriors since the Kamakura period has been overcome and Imperial Government has been restored. We therefore wish that an office of historiography be established, that the good customs of our ancestors be resumed and that knowledge and education be spread throughout the land—and for that purpose We appoint a superintendent. Let us set right the relations between monarch and subject, distinguish clearly between the incongruous and the proper and implant virtue throughout Our land.*[4]

The project was eventually abandoned when the renamed »Office for the Study of History« (*shūshikan*) was transferred in 1888 to the newly established »Tōkyō Imperial University« (*Tōkyō teikoku daigaku*)—the highest learning institution in Japan — and attached to the Faculty of Letters under the name »Historiographical Institute« (*shiryō hensan gakari*), where modern western historical science was put in place.[5] Mehl wrote:

Before the establishment of the Department of History at the Imperial University on 9 September 1887, neither universal history (de facto European and North American history) nor Japanese history were taught as independent subjects. ... At the Imperial University, the first step towards a permanent department of history was taken when the German historian Ludwig Rieß (1861-1928) was appointed professor of history at the University. He took up his post on 3 March 1887 and probably acted as an adviser when the Department of History was established in September 1887. In June 1887 Tsuboi Kumezō [1859-1936] ... was sent to Europe by the Ministry of Education to study history. He studied in Berlin, Prague, Vienna and Zurich, received his PhD from the Imperial University in 1891 and was appointed the second professor at the Department of History when he came home the same year.

The Imperial University now had a department of History and a specialist historian as professor, but Japanese history was still only taught as part of other disciplines, for the Department of History was in fact a department of European history.[6]

After the previous decades of disorder of the 1870s and 1880s with its unhampered westernization, traditional values were gradually reinforced in society and the Imperial state orthodoxy was finally codified in the »Constitution of the Empire of Great Japan« (*Dainihon teikoku kenpō*) that was proclaimed on 11th of February 1889.[7] As Jansen wrote:

The date selected, for the ascension of Jimmu, the sun goddess's grandson, became a national holiday (National Foundation Day), and conveyed the solemnity with which the occasion was designed as both inauguration and continuation. As in 1868, modernity and change were presented as a renewal of antiquity.[8]

The first articles of the *Meiji Constitution* set the tone for the Emperor centered state system that lasted until 1945:

> Article 1. *The Empire of Japan shall be ruled over by a line of Emperors unbroken for ages eternal.*

> Article 4. *The Emperor is the head of the country* (kuni no genshu), *combining in Himself the right to rule* (tōchiken wo sōranshi), *and exercises it, according to the provisions of the present Constitution.* [9]

Together with the »Imperial Rescript of Education« (*kyōiku ni kansuru chokugo*) of 1890, that stressed the value system of 'loyalty' (*chū*) and 'filial piety' (*kō*), both documents codified the dogma of a collectivistic 'family state' (*kazoku kokka*) originating from divine origin in the unbroken Imperial line. The *Imperial Rescript of Education* went as follows:

> *Know ye, Our subjects:*

> *Our Imperial Ancestors have founded Our Empire on a basis broad and everlasting and have deeply and firmly implanted virtue; Our subjects ever united in loyalty and filial piety have from generation to generation illustrated the beauty thereof. This is the glory of the fundamental character of Our Empire, and herein lies the source of Our education.*

> *Ye, Our subjects, be filial to your parents, affectionate to your brothers and sisters; as husbands and wives be harmonious; as friends true; bear yourselves in modesty and moderation; extend your benevolence to all; pursue learning and cultivate arts, and thereby develop intellectual faculties and perfect moral powers; furthermore advance public good and promote common interests; always respect the Constitution and observe the laws; should emergency arise, offer yourselves courageously to the State; and thus guard and maintain the prosperity of Our Imperial Throne coeval with heaven and earth.*

So shall ye not only be Our good and faithful subjects, but render illustrious the best traditions of your forefathers. The Way here set forth is indeed the teaching bequeathed by Our Imperial Ancestors, to be observed alike by Their Descendants and the subjects, infallible for all ages and true in all places. It is Our wish to lay it to heart in all reverence, in common with you, Our subjects, that we may thus attain to the same virtue.[10]

This notion of a special unity between the Japanese Emperor and his people, derived from ancient Shintō myths, was bundled into the term *kokutai* ('national body'), a concept developed since the seventeenth century mainly by scholars of the '*Mito* School' (*Mitogaku*) by combining the Neo-Confucian ethical core of *loyalty* and *filialty* with the Shintō founding myths.[11] In the 1890s, Japanese society converged around this conservative orthodoxy and the acceptance for nonconformist views gradually narrowed.

The academic field remained an open space for new ideas from abroad but a limit for dissenting views was set with the 'Kume Affair' in 1892, when the historian Kume Kunitake (1839-1931) had to resign from Tōkyō Imperial University after publishing an article in which he declared Shintō to be an "outmoded custom deifying nature" (›*Shinto wa saiten no kozoku*‹). Afterwards, scholars avoided to address the Imperial founding myths in their relation to historical facts.[12] Quite the opposite, Kuroita Katsumi (1874-1946) who became professor for ancient Japanese history in 1919, for example treated the Shintō-based *kokutai* myths as quasi-historical events and advocated their validity.[13]

The next generation of historians was even more bound to show reticence challenging the state dogma when Japan entered the phase of high nationalism and war during the 1930s. This group became dominated by Hiraizumi Kiyoshi (1895-1984),[14] a devout believer in the Imperial myths and state structure under the *Meiji Constitution*. Hiraizumi initially adhered to the positivistic research method that was established in the historical field during the Meiji period.[15] But soon he began propagating a historical narrative centered on absolute loyalty to the throne which he based on the devotional self-sacrifice by General Kusunoki Masashige (1294-1336) during the brief 'Kenmu Restoration' (*Kenmu no chūkō*) in Medieval Japan.

Hiraizumi saw his nation's history pervaded by a distinct 'spirit' (*seishin*) of Imperial loyalism which—he believed—sprung into life through Kusunoki's heroism in the fourteenth century and manifested itself again over the following centuries of exemplary courageous deeds of brave men who fought for the Imperial cause: the 'loyalists' (*shishi*) who followed either Yamazaki Ansai (1619-1682) and his '*Kimon* School' (*Kimongaku*) or the *Mito* school that laid the theoretical groundwork for eventually replacing the Tokugawa Shogunate with the modern Imperial state (1868-1945). By praising these activists as the "wise men who came before us" (*sentetsu*), he elevated the loyal death for the Emperor to the highest ideal. As Ueda Kiyoshi wrote: "Like many historians of the Nation's History before 1945, Hiraizumi selectively used a few events and individuals of the medieval history of Japan to provide concrete historical examples of ethical and moral ideologies as navigational devices for the Japanese of his time (the 1930s and 1940s)."[16]

During his academic sojourn abroad in Europe in 1930/1931, Hiraizumi began to sense a looming crisis that his nation soon would have to face. This turned into reality with the 'Manchurian Incident' (*Manshū jihen*) on 18th of September 1931, when Japan entered the 'time of national emergency' (*hijōji*) with the rise of nationalism and militarism that brought Hiraizumi into the forefront as one of its main academic advocates. In 1932, he formed a patriotic student group (*Shukōkai*: 'The Society of Red Light'); two years later he created a private school (*Seiseijuku*: »The Fresh Green Academy«) to teach his disciples—many of them military officers—his ideology of loyalism to the Emperor, while in his university lectures he devalued the French Revolution and its role in modern Western history. The historian Hayashi Kentarō (1913-2004) wrote about Hiraizumi's growing dominance in the university system:

After the retirement of the two academic authorities Kuroita [Katsumi] in 1935 and Tsuji [Zennosuke] in 1938, Dr. Hiraizumi's influence rose rapidly and the Department for Japanese History soon fell under his control. It would have been sufficient if he would have kept his radical right-wing views to himself but this man owned a private academy and nobody became an assistant or obtained a similar scientific position unless he was trained in his academy. It was unfortunate that

Hiraizumi used the university as a public institution for his own purposes. Like [the loyalist] Yoshida Shōin he was consumed by an urge to save the nation. This became more evident as he was promoted by radical right-wing forces. Of course, anyone who didn't comply with his ideology in tests and academic writings didn't receive high grades and wasn't recommended for any employment. ...

There were strict rules among his followers. First, they never addressed each other with the [name suffix] 'kimi/kun'. Because it also pointed [in another usage] to the Emperor and therefore they thought it as being disrespectful when applying it to his subjects. Further, they gave certain historical figures honorific titles, for example Yoshida Shōin had to be called 'Master Yoshida Shōin.' Since Hiraizumi's historical teaching was essentially based on Shintō thought, some Imperial loyalist didn't earn the qualification to be called 'master' (sensei) when they had favored other ideologies along with the Shintō doctrine. 'Master Yamazaki Ansai' was the supreme sensei because he had tried out several theoretical concepts before he finally settled on the Shintō doctrine.[7]

The stiff atmosphere of Hiraizumi's seminars was described by Irokawa Daikichi (1925-2021) who studied briefly under him during the war and later became a pioneer expert on the democratic 'Freedom and People's Rights Movement' *(jiyū minken undō)* of the 1880s that stood in opposition to the autocratic oligarchy who created the *Meiji Constitution* and its top-down power structure that was supported by dogmatists like Hiraizumi. Irokawa portrayed him in a rather unfavorable manner:

Professor Hiraizumi had a cleanliness obsession and washed his hands more than ten times a day. (It was said he performed ritual washings in the toilet.) He was a lean and fussy person with a cold expression. He came to the lecture with a sword and talked only about Kitabatake Chikafusa or the Imperial loyalists. (His lectures had no content and consisted only of his personal views.) Right in the middle of talking he drew the blade and recited its engraving: "The white frost's shade at night when I can't sleep as I worry about the country." [Hiraizumi then exclaimed:]

Another student recalled his own experience with Hiraizumi:

He asked me: "What are the three essential aspects of [the 17th century Mito compilation] »The History of Great Japan« (Dainihonshi)?" Then he thundered at me: "First, the correct genealogy of the Southern Imperial Line! Second, the deletion of the regent Jingū and the adding of Emperor Kōbun! Third, the science that our national history began with Emperor Jinmu!"[9]

The Imperial Army and Navy invited Hiraizumi to speak at their higher training facilities since his ideology backed their privileged role in the Meiji state as being solely responsible to the Emperor as the Commander in Chief. In the unstable first half of the 1930s, when political and social discontent led to demands for a 'Shōwa Restoration' (*Shōwa ishin*) among right wing circles and young officers, he was called to the »Army Academy« (*rikugun shikan gakkō*) to dissuade the cadets from radical ideas that led to several planned and attempted *coup d'état* plots. During the infamous 'February 26 Incident' (*niniroku jiken*) in 1936, when the center of Tōkyō was occupied by rebelling units for three days, Hiraizumi personally convinced Prince Chichibu no miya Yasuhito (1902-1953), the younger brother of the Emperor, not to take a side with the insurgents.

Hiraizumi was acquainted with many high-profile men, for instance Prince Takamatsu no miya Nobuhito (1905-1987), the second sibling of the Emperor, Prince Konoe Fumimaro (1891-1945), the three times Prime Minister from 1937 to 1941, the palace official Kido Kōichi (1889-1977), Tōjō Hideki (1884-1948), the war time Prime Minister from 1941 until 1944, and other generals like Itagaki Seishirō (1885-1948) or Anami Korechika (1887-1945). When Japan entered into the war with China in 1937, Hiraizumi's ties with the military deepened; during the Pacific War he gave many lectures at Army and Navy bases to boost the fighting morale. His historical narrative of being ready to die for the throne at all times provided the ideological base for the *kamikaze* suicide tactic during the second half of the war.

When the capitulation was inevitable, Hiraizumi was approached by a group of officers who rejected any surrender unless the continuance of the Imperial system was assured. This led to the military *coup* attempt on the night of 14-15 August 1945 (*kyūjō jiken*: 'The Imperial Palace Incident'). After the surrender, Hiraizumi resigned from his position as professor at Tōkyō Imperial University and returned to his home town Katsuyama in Fukui Prefecture to become a Shintō priest at his ancestral shrine.

When the US-Occupation ended in 1952, he became a leading voice in conservative circles that sought to revise the constitutional system imposed by the victors and reinstall the prewar value structure. Most notable is his personal connection to Matsudaira Nagayoshi (1915-2005), the man who became head priest of Yasukuni Shrine in 1978 and then enshrined the fourteen Class A War Criminals as 'Shōwa martyrs' (*Shōwa junnansha*) which led to a long-lasting controversy that still affects relationships with Japan's neighboring countries.

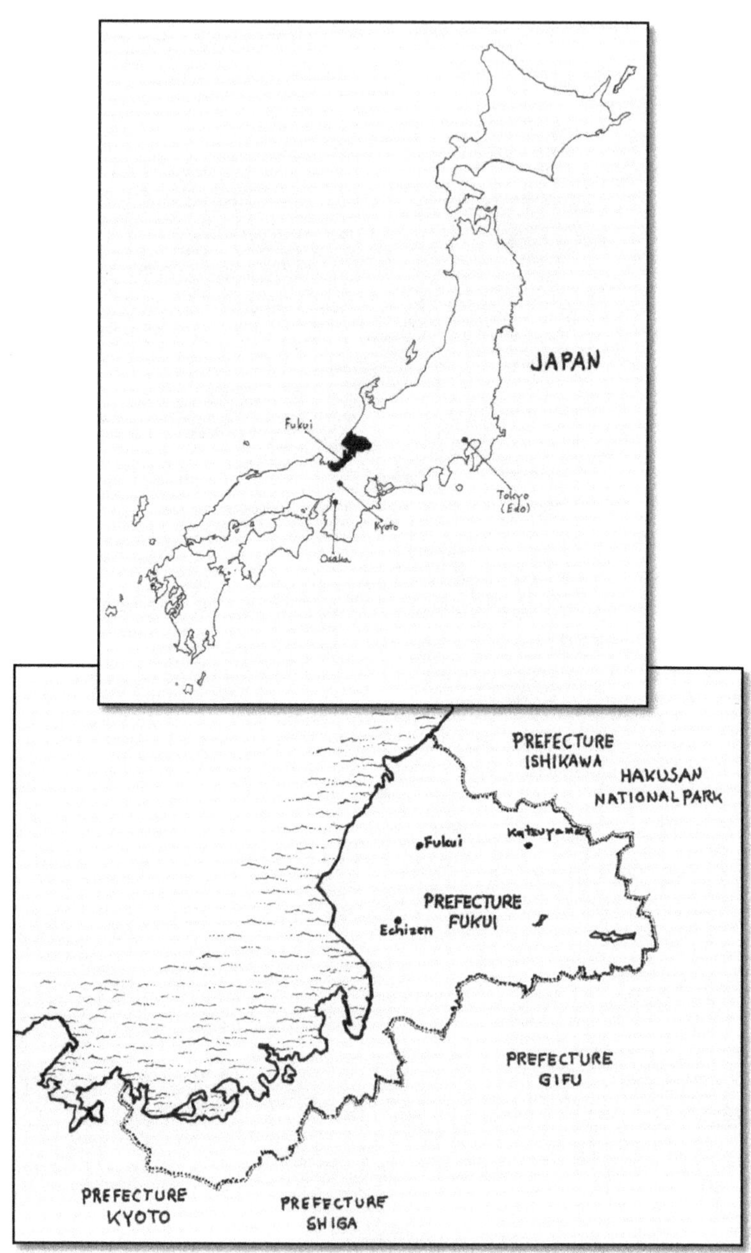

JAPAN
Fukui
Tokyo
(Edo)
Kyoto
Osaka
PREFECTURE
ISHIKAWA
HAKUSAN
NATIONAL PARK
Fukui
Katsuyama
PREFECTURE
FUKUI
Echizen
PREFECTURE
GIFU
PREFECTURE
KYOTO
PREFECTURE
SHIGA

1. *Fukui-Echizen and the 'Kenmu Restoration'*

The historical viewpoint Hiraizumi expressed in his numerous writings and speeches was grounded in his family heritage. His father Hiraizumi Katsugō (1853-1929) was priest at the Hakusan Shrine (*Hakusan jinja*) at the entry path to Mount Hakusan near Heisenji village (*Heisenji mura*, later part of Katsuyama City) in the feudal domain Fukui-Echizen that became Fukui Prefecture in 1871, located around 130 km to the North East of Kyōto.

Mount Hakusan ('The White Mountain', 2,702 m) is one of Japan's 'Three Holy Mountains' (*sanreizan*) along with Mount Tate (3,015 m) in Toyama Prefecture and the eminent Mount Fuji (3,776 m) southwest of Tōkyō. Since ancient times, a distinct Shintō cult called 'Hakusan belief' (*Hakusan shinkō*) spanned the mountain regions bordering the modern prefectures Fukui, Ishikawa and Gifu.[20] The shrine which Katsugō administered in the third generation was linked to the central divine tale in Shintō mythology as it revered the goddess Izanami and the god Ame no Oshihomimi, the father of Ninigi whose mythical great-grandson Jinmu Tennō is said to have descended to Earth to create the Japanese nation around 600 BC.

Until the end of the Edo period, the *Hakusan Shrine* was connected to the *Heisenji* temple that had been the spiritual and administrative center in the area for many centuries. The Buddhist monk Taichō (682-767) founded the temple in 717 near a water spring, hence the name *Heisenji* which means 'Temple at the Tranquil Spring.' When Buddhism was brought to Japan from the mainland in the second half of the first millennial it was common to build Buddhist temples next to native Shintō sites and *Hakusan Shrine* became a symbiotic part of the *Heisenji* areal which grew into a large Buddhist monastery during the Heian period as a branch temple of the dominant Tendai Sect (*Tendaishū*) that shaped Heian Buddhism through its two main temples *Enryakuji* on Mount Hiei in the Imperial capital of Kyōto and *Onjōji* (*Miidera*) in Ōtsu near Kyōto.[21]

With the rise of the warrior culture in the Middle Ages, the *Heisenji* became involved with its large contingents of armed monk soldiers (*sōhei*) on the side of the Taira clan in the 'Battle of Kurikara' in 1183 during the *Genpei* wars.[22] The Taira were defeated and the victorious Minamoto set up the first military government (Shogunate or *Bakufu*) in their eastern base in Kamakura. During the renewed flourishing of Buddhism in the Kamakura era, the Zen-monk Dōgen (1200-1253), who founded the Sōtō Sect (*Sōtōshū*) in Japan, was so impressed by the Hakusan scenery that he built his monastery—'The Temple of Eternal Peace' (*Eiheiji*)—in Echizen with a view at the mountain fifteen kilometers westwards to the *Heisenji*.[23]

The ensuing political events in the fourteenth century were pivotal for Hiraizumi's perception of Japanese history: In 1221, Emperor Gotoba (1180-1239) unsuccessfully tried to overthrow the Kamakura *Bakufu* in the '*Jōkyū* Disturbance' (*Jōkyū no ran*) and was sent into exile to the Oki islands (later Shimane Prefecture). The Mongol invasions in 1274 and 1281 depleted the Shōgun's finances. With the authority of the ruling Hōjō clan in decline Emperor Godaigo (1288-1339) defied the *Bakufu* in the futile 'Genkō Uprising' (*Genkō no ran*, 1331-1333) and was also banished to the Oki region. Meanwhile, his ally, the warrior Kusunoki Masashige together with Godaigo's son Prince Morinaga fought a guerrilla war for the Imperial cause in Kawachi Province (today's Ōsaka), first from his fortification at Akasaka, then at Chihaya:

> *Early in 1333 three large armies left the east, determined to crush Prince Morinaga and Kusunoki Masashige once and for all. At this time the prince was entrenched in a monastery in Yoshino with a defensive force of soldier-monks, while Masashige had established two bases, one at Akasaka and another at Chihaya on Mount Kongō. Since neither Yoshino nor Akasaka was very strong, both soon fell. All three attacking armies then converged upon Kusunoki at Chihaya—a million men,*

according to the Taiheiki. *This figure need not be accepted, but it is clear that the whole strength of the shogunate in the capital area was committed. Nevertheless, the castle held out so stubbornly that it was never breached. It is difficult to exaggerate the importance of Kusunoki's contribution to the eventual success of the imperial arms. By containing the entire strength of the Hōjō, he not only encouraged other rebels to rise, but also prepared the way for the loyalist capture of the virtually undefended capital.*[24]

When Godaigo was able to return to Kyōto, Ashikaga Takauji (1305-1358), the commander of the combined Hōjō forces, turned against the *Bakufu* and allied himself with Godaigo. Kusunoki and Nitta Yoshisada (1301-1338) then marched on Kamakura and destroyed it in the summer of 1333. At the start of the next year Godaigo proclaimed the *Kenmu Restoration* and sought to revive the Imperial system of the Heian period when the Emperor had ruled in person.[25]

Godaigo soon faced problems as discontent grew among the feudal clans because he didn't reward them with land titles as they had expected. After quelling a Hōjō insurgence in Kamakura in 1335, Takauji took the title Shōgun ('Supreme General'), which Godaigo had bestowed upon his sons, for himself and awarded land grants to his vassals in defiance of the Emperor who sent Nitta with an army to 'punish' him. Takauji defeated Nitta and occupied Kyōto in the early months of 1336 but was forced to pull back to Kyūshū where he fought Godaigo's allies, the Kikuchi clan. When he again marched on Kyōto, Godaigo instructed Kusunoki to fight him in a field battle. Kusunoki, knowing that his small forces had no chances to win, obeyed the order and headed into defeat in the 'Battle at the Minato River' (*Minatogawa no tatakai*). Surrounded by Takauji's forces, he committed suicide together with his brother after pledging "to return seven times to kill the traitors." Masashige's head was cut off and brought to Takauji while his body was buried in a mass grave.[26]

Takauji established his own Shogunate in Kyōto (the Muromachi *Bakufu*, 1336-1573) but Godaigo refused to give up and retreated into the mountains of Yoshino. Takauji installed a rivaling Emperor in Kyōto—the 'Northern Court' (*hokuchō*)—to delegitimize Godaigo's 'Southern Court' (*nanchō*) that held out in Yoshino. Ivan Morris laid out the reasons why the *Kenmu Restoration* had failed:

[T]he Restoration never had the slightest chance of working. Failure was inherent in its very concept. Godaigo's ideal of going "back to Engi," that is, to the supposedly benign conditions that prevailed in the early tenth century, could only be a fantasy. Most of the high-ranking nobles proved to be helpless in dealing with economic matters that had long been the responsibility of the Bakufu, and in the Records Office and similar departments the government was increasingly obliged to use warrior personnel even though this contravened the ideal of aristocratic rule. The nobility had long since lost the power and the ability to govern and could continue existing only by the tolerance of the military whom they so blatantly scorned. Thus the only significant question in fourteenth-century Japan was not whether government would be in the hands of the aristocracy or of the warrior class but what particular form the new military rule would take.

Godaigo's policy was not only a total anachronism but showed that he had never understood why so many members of the warrior class had swung to his side and restored him to power. In the case of a few remarkable individuals like Masashige and Yoshisada, this support may indeed have betokened an upsurge of loyalist spirit; but most of the warriors had sided with him because of dissatisfaction with a particular military regime. As Takauji knew very well, he and his fellow warriors had not destroyed the Kamakura Bakufu in order to restore power to the Court but to further their own objectives, and in the long run few of them would back an imperial government, however legitimate, if it ignored their demands. In obstinately clinging to the illusion that loyalism rather than self-interest was the guiding motive of his warriors—an illusion that was undoubtedly fostered by men like [Kitabatake] Chikafusa and Masashige—Godaigo misread both the spirit of the times and human nature in general. He thus doomed himself and his handful of true supporters to ultimate collapse.[27]

Echizen Province initially had supported the *Kenmu Restoration* because its governor (*shugo*) Shiba Takatsune (1305-1367) was a related vassal of the Ashikaga. His forces then fought together with Takauji against Kusunoki at the Minato River. As Godaigo fled Kyōto, Nitta and two Imperial Princes moved northwards to secure Echizen. In 1337, Shiba took Nitta's fortifications at Kanegasaki. Nitta was killed the next year while besieging Shiba's 'Black Fortress' (*Kuromaru*). The *Heisenji* monk warriors were first aligned with Nitta but switched sides and the temple compound was destroyed in the fighting in 1338 and again in 1340. It was rebuilt and became the Ashikaga's administrative center for the Hokuriku region. The split loyalties in Echizen during this era are exemplified by a grave stone for Kusunoki in the pine forest near *Hakusan Shrine*. According to the source *Reiōzan Heisenji Engi*, the epitaph was erected by Kusunoki's nephew—a *Heisenji* monk with the name Eshū—who saw his uncle in a vision during a Buddhist *nenbutsu* recitation around the time when he died at the Minato River. Kusunoki appeared on his horse before Eshū in the prayer hall and said to him:

I fought for the Emperor with all my strength but the battle's fortune was not in

my favor and I finally closed my eyes forever at Minato River in Settsu Province.[28]

Kusunoki's son Masatsura (1326-1348), who organized the Yoshino defenses, sent some of his father's personal items to the *Heisenji*, including a sword that was said to be buried under the stone in the forest.[29] Godaigo died in 1339 and was succeeded by his son, Emperor Gomurakami (1328-1368). Meanwhile in Tsukuba (Ibaraki Prefecture), the court noble Kitabatake Chikafusa (1293-1354) and his forces held an area around Oda castle. While under siege by Ashikaga allies, he wrote between 1338 and 1341 the treatise *Jinnō shōtōki* (»The Chronicles of the Authentic Lineages of the Divine Emperors«) to give legitimacy to Gomurakami and his task to unite the realm under Imperial rule. Kitabatake based the *Jinnō shōtōki* on the Shintō mythology from the *Nihon shoki* by declaring Japan to be the 'Land of the Gods' (*shinkoku*):

Great Japan is the Land of the Gods. The heavenly progenitor founded it, and the

sun goddess bequeathed it to her descendants to rule eternally. Only in our country

is this true; there are no similar examples in other countries. This is why our country

is called the divine land.[30]

The 'Period of the Southern and Northern Imperial Courts' (*nanbokuchō jidai*) ended in 1392 when the Court eventually united in Kyōto under control of the Ashikaga *Bakufu*. Andrew Goble explains why the *Southern Court* was able to withstand in Yoshino for over fifty years:

> *This Nanbokuchō (Northern and Southern Courts) conflict continued as long as it did because of four inseparable factors. First, the ongoing existence of two rival branches of the imperial family not only provided the opportunity to mask any action as being in accord with legitimate authority, but simultaneously also vitiated the notion of supreme and legitimate central authority. Second, the post-Kamakura warrior class, apart from the Ashikaga, was focused on carving out new regional power, and so what we call the civil war was in reality a decentralized, self-perpetuating conflict carried out under the rubric of support for either of the imperial lines. Third, while the Ashikaga claimed a national presence, it essentially depended on regional warriors for military resources and thus could really establish hegemony only through proxy. That proxy came at a considerable price: regional figures, appointing themselves as military constables, appropriated up to half of any tax or production formally destined for Kyoto proprietors, which of course strengthened their hands even more. Fourth, as an inevitable consequence of these factors, a military solution to the civil war was impossible.*[31]

In the late fourteenth century, the events surrounding the *Kenmu Restoration* were written down in the colorful epic tale *Taiheiki* (»The Chronicle of the Great Peace«) by an unknown author, probably a Buddhist monk.[32] Kusunoki, the *Taiheiki*'s main hero, over the centuries became the popular figure 'Lord Camphor Tree' (*Nankō*):[33]

> *Masashige's posthumous popularity was slow to develop. Following his suicide at Minato River the grieving Godaigo (who was, of course, largely responsible for the disaster) promoted Masashige to the Third Rank; but, after the final victory of the Ashikagas, members of the Kusunoki family were for a long time held in low repute, being regarded as fire-brands and disturbers of the new order. It was not*

until the sixteenth century that the general attitude towards Masashige began to shift decisively in his favour: in 1563 he was officially accorded a posthumous pardon, and thereafter his rise was rapid. This is related to the growing fame of "The Chronicle of the Great Peace," which, despite its modest literary merits, became established as one of the most popular and influential books in Japan. Its supreme hero is Kusunoki Masashige, and its best-loved passages are those that describe his tragic career.[34]

After the 'Ōnin War' (*Ōnin no ran*) 1467-1477, the Ashikaga lost their power and Japan split up into various warring domains (*sengoku jidai*). The *Heisenji* in Echizen was completely destroyed in 1574 during a local uprising (*ikkō ikki*) after which the temple compound was abandoned and only few buildings remained. When Tokugawa Ieyasu (1543-1616) unified the country, Fukui-Echizen became a feudal Domain (*Fukui han*) ruled by one of his sons, Yūki Hideyasu (1574-1607) who took the surname Matsudaira in 1604. The Matsudaira administrated Fukui as 'Lords related to the Shōgun' (*shinpan daimyō*) through the Edo period. Because of the Shogunate's difficulties with Hideyasu's son Matsudaira Tadanao (1595-1650), who couldn't solve an armed conflict with one of his retainers, the area around Katsuyama castle was separated from Fukui in 1623 and became the Katsuyama Domain (*Katsuyama han*) ruled by the Ogasawara clan who kept close ties with the Matsudaira.[35]

During the Edo period, Neo-Confucianism (*Shushigaku*) in the tradition of the Chinese philosopher Zhu Xi (1130-1200) served as the legitimizing doctrine for the Tokugawa Shōgun who ordered the scholar Hayashi Razan (1583-1657) to write an official historical description of Japan, »The Comprehensive Mirror of this Land« (*Honchō tsugan*) that was completed in 1670 by his son Gahō (1618-1680). Razan had to tackle with the question which one of the two Imperial courts in the fourteenth century was the legitimate one. He decided in favor of Godaigo's *Southern Court* which possessed the Imperial regalia during the schism.[36] The revaluation of the *Southern Court* in the eyes of Edo historians converged with the growing public sentiment for Kusunoki:

During the Tokugawa period there was increasing sympathy with the "southern" cause. Respect for its self-sacrificing adherent, Masashige, reached such a pitch that it became known as nankō sūhai (*"the worship of Lord Kusunoki"). Eminent Confucianists described him as an exemplar of the most important moral virtues, and the famous scholar-statesman Arai Hakuseki elevated him to a higher level than Emperor Godaigo himself.*[37]

The dogmatic veneration for Kusunoki began with Yamazaki Ansai whose intellectual journey brought him to a synthesis of the Neo-Confucian ethics with the ancient Shintō myths which, according to him, laid the 'way' for everybody to follow in the 'Land of the Gods' as stated in the *Jinnō shōtōki*. Yamazaki founded a Shintō branch called *Suika Shintō* that worshiped the Sun-Goddess Amaterasu Ōmikami and her offspring, the Imperial line. He elevated the reverence (*kei*) for the Emperor in the combination of Shintō and Neo-Confucian values to supreme virtue. Yamazaki adored Kusunoki who dutifully obeyed the Emperor's wish despite his personal reservations and took his own life on the battlefield after he had obliged his son Masatsura to follow his example. This became the ideal in Yamazaki's *Kimon* school. Wakabayashi Kyōsai (1679-1732), for example, named his Kyōto academy the 'House longing for Camphor' (*Bōnanken*).[38]

Tokugawa Mitsukuni (1628-1701), the head of the *Mito* Domain (later Ibaraki Prefecture), ordered the compilation of a comprehensive historical chronicle that also combined Neo-Confucianism with the ancient tales about the divine descendance of the Imperial line. »The History of Great Japan« (*Dainihonshi*) initially spanned from the legendary first Emperor Jinmu until Godaigo, but Mitsukuni also added the Period of the Southern and Northern Courts (1336-1392) and determined the *Southern Court* to be the legitimate one based on the *Jinnō shōtōki*. He visited Kusunoki's death site (in modern day Kōbe) and set up a memorial stone with the inscription "Ah, the grave of the loyal vassal Kusunoki" (*Aa chūshin Nanshi no haka*).[39] The *Mito* school further fused Imperial loyalism with the Neo-Confucian values and laid the way for modern Japanese nationalism as the historian John Brownlee wrote:

It is strange that one of the most powerful statements of imperial loyalism came from a branch family of the Tokugawa, which was the hereditary ruling family of the bakufu. It took the form of a history, Dai Nihon Shi, *begun by Tokugawa*

In Fukui-Echizen, the memory of Kusunoki and the *Kenmu Restoration* was kept alive during the Edo era. In 1656, peasants found an old samurai helmet at *Kuromaru* in Echizen where Nitta had died in an ambush in 1338. Matsudaira Mitsumichi (1636-1674), the fourth *daimyō* of Fukui, determined it to be Nitta's helmet and ordered the construction of a tomb on the site. In 1662, he also built a granite balustrade around Kusunoki's grave stone in the *Heisenji* forest to honor him.[41] The American William E. Griffis (1843-1928), who came to Fukui as a teacher on the invitation of the last *daimyō* Matsudaira Yoshinaga (Matsudaira Shungaku, 1828-1890), noted the reverence for Nitta in the region:

The tomb of this brave man stands, carefully watched and tended, near Fukui, in Echizen, hard by the very spot where he fell. I often passed it in my walks, when living in Fukui in 1871, and noticed that fresh blooming flowers were almost daily laid upon it—the tribute of an admiring people. A shrine and monument in memoriam were erected in his native place during the year 1875.[42]

Griffis equally observed the strong devotion for Kusunoki:

Of all the characters in Japanese history, that of Kusunoki Masashigé stands pre-eminent for pureness of patriotism, unselfishness of devotion to duty, and calmness of courage. The people speak of him in tones of reverential tenderness, and, with an admiration that lacks fitting words, behold in him the mirror of stainless loyalty. I have more than once asked my Japanese students and friends whom they considered the noblest character in their history. Their unanimous answer was "Kusunoki Masashigé." Every relic of this brave man is treasured up with religious care; and fans inscribed with poems written by him, in fac-simile of his handwriting, are sold in the shops and used by those who burn to imitate his exalted patriotism.[43]

Matsudaira Yoshinaga became involved in the political debate that erupted after the arrival of Commodore Perry's 'Black Ships' in Edo in 1853. First, he supported a group of local *Kimon* acitivists around Hashimoto Keigaku (Hashimoto Sanai, 1834-1859) and asked him in 1855 to lead Fukui's new academy—»The School for the Illumination of the Way« (*Meidōkan*)—where 'Practical Learning' (*jitsugaku*) was combined with the study of *Kimon* and *Mito* teachings. *Meidōkan*'s main scholar Yoshida Tōkō (1808-1875) began a letter exchange with Fujita Tōko (1806-1855), the head of the Mito *Kōdōkan* academy, who advocated the xenophobic doctrine of 'Revere the Emperor and Expel the Foreigners' (*sonnō jōi*). Yoshinaga then sent Hashimoto to work with Saigō Takamori (1827-1877) from Satsuma to promote the Imperial cause. Hashimoto was eventually arrested during the '*Ansei* Purges' (*Ansei no taigoku*) in 1859, when the Shogunate cracked down on the opposition. He was decapitated at the age of twenty-five and became a modern hero figure in Fukui-Echizen.[44]

Yoshinaga was deposed as *daimyō* in Fukui during the *Ansei* Purges but was reinstated afterwards. In 1862, he worked towards an alliance between Court and *Bakufu* (*kōbu gattai*). In 1863, he planned to march with his samurai to Kyōto to seize the Imperial palace. In 1867, he tried to form a short-lived council assembly to mediate between the disintegrating Shogunate and the advancing Imperial movement.[45] After the *Meiji Restoration* in 1868, he joined the new government for a year but returned to Fukui where he strengthened the Shintō religion when it was separated from Buddhism (*haibutsu kishaku*) in a violent movement that occurred all over Japan. Yoshinaga built a local »Shrine to Invite the Souls« (*Shōkonsha*) for the men who died for the Imperial cause. The main *Shōkonsha* in Tōkyō was renamed in 1869 to *Yasukuni jinja* (»Shrine for Peace in the Country«) and became the sanctuary for the enshrinement of the war dead.[46]

On the grave site for Kusunoki in Kōbe that Tokugawa Mitsukuni had set up, the Minatogawa Shrine (*Minatogawa jinja*) was built in 1872 as one of the 'Fifteen Shrines of the *Kenmu* Restoration' (*Kenmu chūko jūgosha*). Every year in May, a 'Kusunoki Festival' (*Nankōsai*) and a parade were celebrated at the Shrine. An imposing bronze statue of Kusunoki was erected in front of the Imperial palace in Tōkyō in the year 1900. In 1911, a public controversy erupted around the question which one of the two Imperial Courts in the fourteenth century held genuine legitimacy (*Nanbokuchō seijunron*) and a consensus was enforced in favor of Godaigo's *Southern Court*:[47]

The Southern-Northern Courts controversy in 1911 is generally seen as reinforcing the taboo on discussion about the imperial house. In 1892 Kume Kunitake had been alone in his brush with authority and got no support from his fellow historians. They thought he was intemperate. In 1911 all the leading professional historians were involved, even though they were intemperate, and they learned the depth of public feeling about the imperial house and the extent of state power. The unsettling experience seems to have recalled them to a sense of their position as Japanese citizens and servants of the state. Employed in the imperial university, they had no business contradicting government decisions about education. All of them thenceforth accepted a distinction between education [kyōiku], under which

Matsudaira Yoshinaga's third son Yoshitami (1882-1948) studied from 1896 until 1908 in Great Britain at the University of Oxford. After his return to Japan, he served in the military and then entered the Ministry of the Imperial Household (*kunaishō*) in 1912 as a career bureaucrat. He led one branch (*bunke*) of the Matsudaira family and was granted the noble title of Viscount (*shishaku*) that initially was awarded to his father for his contributions leading up to the Meiji Restoration. Matsudaira Yoshitami became Hiraizumi's mentor in Tōkyō.

1. 1. Studying History at Tōkyō Imperial University

Hiraizumi was born on 16 February 1895 in Katsuyama (Fukui Prefecture) as the only son of the Shintō priest Hiraizumi Katsugō along with three sisters. His mother Sadako was the daughter of a samurai from the former Katsuyama feudal Domain. The spelling of the surname Hiraizumi is the Japanese *kun*-reading of the two Chinese characters *Heisen* ('tranquil water spring'); his given name Kiyoshi ('clear') used the same character (*on*-reading: *chō*) as the monk Taichō who founded the *Heisenji* in the eighth century. The *Hakusan Shrine* was separated from the *Heisenji* ground in 1871 as were many other Shintō Shrines that had been connected to Buddhist temples for more than a thousand years. The old wooden mansion (*genjōin*) built in 1778, which had been the *Heisenji* administrator's office, became the residence of the Hiraizumi family.[49]

During the war against Imperial Russia 1904-1905 Hiraizumi was full of patriotism. At the age of twelve an uncle gave him a printed *Jinnō shōtōki* edition which he compared to the old handwritten *Jinnō shōtōki* version dating from 1531 that belonged to his father's shrine—this sparked his interest in historical science. (Several *Jinnō shōtōki* versions exist; the original text, that Kitabatake had sent to Emperor Gomurakami, was lost.) Hiraizumi favored reading nationalistic *Mito* works and reported a teacher who allegedly had criticized the Imperial House. In 1911 during middle school, he compiled a chronology of the *Hakusan* deities, followed by a historical survey on the *Heisenji*.[50] In 1912 he came to the prestigious »Fourth Higher School« (*daishi kōtō gakkō*) in Kanazawa, whose principal gave him a book set of Hashimoto Keigaku's writings (*Hashimoto Sanai zenshū*) which he read with much interest.[51]

The *Fourth Higher School* was one of the four nationwide preparation schools for selecting the applicants to enter Tōkyō Imperial University, Japan's most esteemed university. Hiraizumi enrolled there in the fall of 1915 in the field of 'Japanese Medieval History' (*chūseishi*) as part of the 'Department for Japanese History' (*kokushi gakka*). In 1917, as he became the leader of the university's 'Fourth Higher School Alumni Student Circle' he insisted on its members' adherence to the official dogma of 'statism' (*kokka shugi*) — meaning allegiance to the Imperial state and its oligarchic-autocratic structure.[52] When the Russian monarchy was toppled during the October Revolution he wrote a patriotic poem:

> *Even when my body passes away*
> *And my family perishes,*
> *I sacrifice myself ardently for Our Country.*[53]

He published his first academic articles.[54] His graduation thesis *Chūsei ni okeru shaji to shakai to no kankei* (»Shrines and temples in the Middle Ages and their role in society«) was highly evaluated by his professor Kuroita Katsumi. When Hiraizumi graduated in March 1918, Matsudaira Yoshinaga offered him a promising position in the Imperial Household but Hiraizumi followed Kuroita's advice to pursue an academic path at the university. In the autumn of 1918, he joined a research project to examine the documents related to the *Tōshōgū* mausoleum in Nikkō dedicated to Tokugawa Ieyasu, the founder of the Tokugawa Shogunate.[55]

As the First World War in Europe ended, social unrest caused by rising food prices erupted in Japan. This led to the first parliamentary based government formed on 28 September 1918 by Hara Takashi (1856-1921), the head of the largest political party *Rikken Seiyūkai*. In 1919, a wave of liberal and socialist thoughts swept the intellectual and academic circles and Japan entered into the liberal decade named 'Taishō Democracy.' Conservatives were dismayed by the open rejection of the *kokutai* state dogma that had dominated the nation for three decades. The reactionary front trying to reverse the ideological trends among students was led by professor Uesugi Shinkichi (1878-1929), a hardliner who also came from Fukui, who ascribed unlimited authority to the

Emperor by placing him above the Meiji Constitution. In September 1919, Uesugi formed a patriotic student movement with the support of Kuroita and other conservative academics, the 'Student Association of Comrades to Strengthen the Country' (*Kōkoku dōshikai*).[56]

Hiraizumi joined the *Kōkoku dōshikai* that began agitating against the assistant professor Morito Tatsuo (1888-1984) from the Economics Department who had published an article about the Russian anarchist and revolutionary Pyotr Alexeyevich Kropotkin (1842-1921). As a result of the defamation, the Home Ministry (*naimushō*) banned the article and Morito was suspended in January 1920 to be eventually sentenced to three months in jail. The *Kōkoku dōshikai*'s triumphant behavior resulted in harsh criticism against the group, after which most members left except for a small core. Kishi Nobusuke (1896-1987), the later Prime Minister from 1957 to 1960, who had studied law under Uesugi, claimed that Hiraizumi had tried to convince him to stay in the group. The *Kōkoku dōshikai* disbanded but its ties to other patriotic lineups continued. In 1920, Hiraizumi met the activist Ōkawa Shūmei (1886-1957) who took him to a gathering for the anti-British Indian exile Rash Behari Bose (1886-1945), organized by the right-wing group 'The Black Ocean Society' (*Genyōsha*).[57]

At Tōkyō Imperial University Hiraizumi became in charge of editing the unpublished papers of professor Tanaka Yoshinari (1860-1919) who had passed away the year before.[58] In October 1921 Hiraizumi married Hayako, the daughter of Morishita Tatsunosuke, director of the Gramophone company *Nittō chikuonki*.[59] In March 1923, he became a lecturer (*kōshi*) for Japanese history (*kokushi*) and held courses about the Japanese Middle Ages including a seminar on the *Azuma kagami* (»Mirror of the East«), a chronicle from the Kamakura period. On September 1st 1923, the powerful Kantō Earthquake struck the capital. Many university buildings were destroyed, including the 'Historical Archive' (*shiryō hensan gakari*) where the Department for Japanese History was located. During the reconstruction of the campus the department was placed in a new building in 1925 by which its academic standing was elevated, but the 'Department of Western History' (*seiyōshi gakka*) remained the university's main historical section.[60]

1. 2. Embracing the 'Japanese Spirit'

Up until the year 1925 Hiraizumi followed the positivistic historical research method developed by the German historian Leopold von Ranke (1795-1886) that had been instituted at Tōkyō Imperial University in 1887 by Ranke's disciple Ludwig Riess who led the History Faculty until 1901.[61] But Hiraizumi began rejecting this methodology, whose "emphasis on peoples and epochs," as he saw it, "correlates with the democratic trend" of the Western nations and also would lead to Marxist historical materialism which he denied both to be applicable to Japan.[62] He referred to the book *Theory & History of Historiography* by the Italian historian philosopher Benedetto Croce (1866-1952) that at that time was translated into Japanese by Hani Gorō (1901-1983) in the Department for Japanese History.[63] Croce missed in the source-based positivistic approach the final 'truth' in history. Likewise, Hiraizumi started to argue for a "subjectivistic selection of the truth among the facts." He claimed that "spiritual truth doesn't exist objectively" but "must be discerned by choosing it in its relation to the whole":

The scholarly approach since the Meiji era puts almost all of its focus on finding the facts (jitsu). *This is called scientific research. Its method is analysis. But analysis is dismantlement; and dismantlement means death. The opposite is unification by searching for the truth* (shin). *Unification is life. But this reflects art rather than science. Ultimately it becomes faith. … It goes without saying that a sober scientific attitude and meticulous research are both necessary. But if history is only analyzed in such a way it dies. What brings history to life and what causes it to continue is the mysterious spiritual strength* (reikon no chikara) *of the people who live the faith of their history. Through this spiritual strength facts become the truth. What the historian should search for is precisely this truth. Only by so doing*

he becomes the master over the past, present and future and can be of value in the

development of the world.[64]

He presented his thoughts to the public in an article for the journal *Taiyō* in January 1926.[65] In April 1926 he was granted the academic doctor title for his previously submitted thesis *Chūsei ni okeru shaji to shakai to no kankei* and promoted to assistant professor. He quickly published two books, *Chūsei ni okeru seishin seikatsu* (»The Spiritual Life in the Middle Ages«)[66] and a collection of his articles under the title *Waga rekishikan* (»My View about History«),[67] followed by an academic text about the *Keiranshū yōshū* (»The leaf collection from the valley storm«) written by the Buddhist monk Kōsō (1276-1350).[68] In November 1926 Hiraizumi printed a revised version of his thesis *Chūsei ni okeru shaji to shakai to no kankei* as required for the doctor title after the German academic model.[69]

Hiraizumi began promoting the loyalist heritage from his home province Fukui. He became active in the 'Society in Keigaku's Memory' (*Keigakukai*) that had been founded in 1902 and published the book volumes *Hashimoto Sanai zenshū* in 1908. In October 1926 he encouraged Hatta Yūjirō (1849-1930), a former Navy Captain from Fukui and member in the House of Commons (*shugi'in*) from 1912 to 1917, to become its first president. Hiraizumi organized *Keigakukai*'s program that included regular speeches and an annual memorial ceremony at Hashimoto's grave in Tōkyō. He also helped restarting the 'Fukui Society' (*Fukuikai*) in Tōkyō that was renamed to 'Fukui Club' (*Fukui Kurabu*) under Hatta's chairmanship. Hiraizumi further functioned as dean of the *Hojinkai* residence for students from Fukui, where he implemented strict rules to honor the loyalist tradition.[70]

As a strong traditionalist who upheld the official *kokutai* doctrine as propagated through the state's institutions, Hiraizumi supported the existing power structure with its ruling class and social hierarchy. He reacted negatively to debates in patriotic groups about the necessity for wide-ranging reforms (*kakushin*) to solve the discrepancy in society and forge the nation together. Advocates of the 'reform right-wing' (*kakushin uyoku*) often referred to the »Outline Plan for the Reorganization of Japan« (*Nihon kaizō hōan taikō,* written by the revolutionary Kita Ikki (1883-1937) in 1919, that merged leftist and rightist ideas and even called for the suspension of the Meiji Constitution.[71] Brian J. McVeigh summarized the two right-wing factions in prewar Japan:

> *Many scholars have divided Japan's fundamentalist nationalisms into two more or less competing strains: reactionary traditionalism and movements that resembled European forms of fascism. The former is associated with "pure Japanism"* (junsui nippon-shugi) *and "emperorism"* (kōdō-shugi), *the latter with Japan-centric renovationism and national socialism* (kokka shakai-shugi *or* kokumin shakai-shugi). *Though the distinction was not always clear-cut, Japanese scholars have distinguished between "ideological right-wing"* (kannen uyoku) *and "organizational right-wing"* (soshiki uyoku), *the former referring to "pure Japanism" and the latter national socialism.*[72]

Hiraizumi stressed that reforms in Japan must reflect the 'spirit of its history' and be in accordance with 'Emperor Jinmu's founding directive' (*Jinmu tennō sōgyō*) 2600 years ago, meaning it could be initiated solely by the Emperor. Historically, Hiraizumi claimed, the first such renewal (*kakushin*) in line with the founding decree had been the 'Taika Reforms' (*Taika no kaishin*) in the year 645 after which the Court ordered the compilation of the *Kojiki* and *Nihon shoki* "to codify the ancient mandate." The peak of Imperial rule under the Emperors Daigo (885-930) and Murakami (926-967) in the Heian period, he continued, became the reform model for Gotoba and Godaigo to regain their authority, which led Kitabatake to affirm the "ancestors' eternal mandate" in the *Jinnō shōtōki*. He concluded that the *Meiji Restoration* was in full accord with the ancient directive and any further reforms could only happen by Imperial decree.[73]

In an essay written in June 1927, ›*Kokushigaku no kotsuzui*‹ (›The mark of our National Historiography‹), Hiraizumi laid out the theoretical frame on which he based all of his future work. He sent the text to Ōkawa who just published his own lectures as a book titled *Nippon seishin kenkyū* (»Research of the Japanese Spirit«).[74] Ōkawa was very appreciative of Hiraizumi's thesis who declared that history "isn't just the mere passing of time" but the "manifestation of an inherit spirit" carried out by awakened men whose character, consciousness and will are all led by this spirit, while for normal people history remains a "simple background" with no connotations. History in Japan therefore must always mean a 'revival' (*fukkatsu*) to protect and nurture the continuing revelation of this 'National Spirit' (*Nippon seishin*) that was created together with the ancient state by Emperor Jinmu and shaped it from the *Taika Reforms* until the end of the Heian era. It reappeared—so Hiraizumi's thesis—in the *Kenmu* period, was then conceptually confirmed through the *Jinnō shōtōki* and *Dainihonshi*, and finally became the driving force leading up to the Meiji Restoration:

> *With the publication of the* Jinnō shōtōki, *the national foundation spirit was firmly revived. It was further transmitted in the* Dainihonshi *until it spread by the end of the Bakufu among the whole population and allowed the large undertaking of the Meiji Renewal to be implemented. The* Jinnō shōtōki, *this one book, carried the [Japanese] state and forms... the axis of Our National History.*[75]

Hiraizumi didn't devalue the religious and cultural impact of Buddhism on Japan and its history, but as a result of his upbringing in a Shintō Shrine household he laid emphasis on the Shintō legacy and agreed with its forceful decoupling from Buddhist temples after the Meiji Restoration because "Buddhism has blocked the *kokutai* revival."[76] Hiraizumi based his historical hypothesis on the assumption of an *eternal spiritual substance* that was sparked into existence in the mythical age. But he also made out several 'formative phases' of this spirit, for which he cited Croce: "To think about history is certainly to divide it into periods." Hiraizumi listed five 'cultural phases' of the *Japanese Spirit* when modes and ideals in the country had changed:

1. The 'Ancient Age' (*kodai*) which, untouched from the outside, was marked by 'purity' (*junsui*).
2. The 'Age of the Gods' (*kamiyo*) or 'Age of Commencement' (*jōdai*) from the Asuka/Nara period to the Heian era that installed the 'ideal' (*risō*) with its quest for 'beauty' (*bi*) in architecture, literature and art.

3. The 'Middle Ages' (*chūsei*) when the *ideal* was interrupted with the ascent of the warrior clans, while Buddhism brought a cultural peak in its search for the 'holy' (*sei*).
4. The 'Premodern Age' (*kinsei*) when Buddhism was rejected in the desire for the high principle of the ethical and moral 'good' (*zen*).
5. The 'Modern times' (*gendai*) which bring scientific clearance about the historical 'truth' (*shin*).[77]

He declared:

When one has a grasp of the particularities of a state and perceives the particularities of each period, the man would reach the deepest in terms of historical consciousness. Furthermore, regardless of the changes from one period to the next, one will become the man who will truly live inside history by becoming able to inherit the Spirit (seishin) *that absolutely runs through from the beginning to the end [of history].*[78]

Hiraizumi expanded on his 'cultural history' for a while.[79] But he had no interest in ethnological and anthropological studies as illustrated by an episode in the summer of 1928 when the student Nakamura Kichiji (1905-1986), who later became history professor at »Tōhoku Imperial University« (*Tōhoku teikoku daigaku*), visited him with his outline for his graduation thesis. Hearing Nakamura's proposal to research "the history of the peasants", he reacted disdainfully in anger: "Do peasants have a history? Do pigs have a history?"[80]

For Hiraizumi nothing could supersede the loftiness of the spirit of loyalty towards the Emperor which he perceived in its purest form in Kusunoki's heroism. From this 'seminal event' he constructed a spiritual genealogy of *Kimon* and *Mito* activism in the Edo era when "spirit imbued individuals" like Yoshida Shōin (1830-1859) and Hashimoto Keigaku opened the path to the Meiji Restoration. In July 1928, he participated in an event for the '300th Birth Anniversary of Tokugawa Mitsukuni' that subsequently lit up an increasing scholarly interest in the *Mito* School, as Rieko Kamei-Dyche sums up the assessment of the historian Yoshida Toshizumi:

Almost nothing existed in terms of dedicated scholarship on Mitogaku before the 1930s. Earlier Taishō-era works on Mitogaku were published, but achieved little notice, and few are extant. Often we can only deduce the existence of such works from authors who in later publications made reference to their early work. A broader consciousness of Mitogaku appears to have been nonexistent. ... According to Yoshida's overview, there was nothing before 1928. That year was the 300th anniversary of the birth of Tokugawa Mitsukuni, the Daimyō of Mito who initiated the great historical project for which the early Mito school was most famous. In light of the positive evaluation of Mitsukuni during the prewar era, it is not particularly surprising that from the anniversary date onward there was a renewed interest in Mito. Over the next few years, Mitogaku studies began to become more popular, and gradually scholarly works on the subject began to appear.[81]

Hiraizumi focused his own research on the works of Kuriyama Senpō (1671-1706) and Tani Jinzan (Tani Shigetō, 1663-1718) who both had studied under Yamazaki and his disciple Asami Keisai (1652-1712). Kuriyama argued in his »Hōken Chronicle« (*Hōken taiki*) in 1689 that the loss of Imperial power in the twelfth century had been caused by an absence of virtue on the side of the throne. This reasoning led the *Mito* scholars around Mitsukuni—who in 1692 called Kuriyama to his research group to compile the *History of Great Japan*—to the conclusion that *vice versa* a strong manifestation of Imperial virtue would expose the illegitimacy of the Shōgun's rule. Hiraizumi saw this as an essential perceptual step for the subsequent development of the loyalist movement that eventually toppled the *Bakufu* and restored Imperial power.[82]

He presented his spiritual concept in an NHK radio lecture in November 1928, just before the enthronement ceremony for Hirohito (1901-1989) who had become Emperor after his father Yoshihito's (1879-1926) death.[83] Hiraizumi's radio appearance spurred the interest of Admiral Arima Ryōkitsu (1861-1944), the chairman of the 'Naval Ex-servicemen Association' (*kaigun yūshūkai*). After serving in the Combined Fleet during the Russo-Japanese War, Arima led the »Imperial Navy Academy« (*kaigun heigakkō*) from 1914 to 1916 and retired from active service in 1922. He revered Yamazaki Ansai, whose grave in Kyōto he had found overgrown with weeds in 1912 and ordered it to be cleaned. Arima invited Hiraizumi to the *Yūshūkai* to talk about Yamazaki. Hiraizumi made the topic of his presentation the "transcendental power that pervades our history":

> *The vigorous promulgation of the gods' will began with the* Jinnō shōtōki. *Ansai's patriotic thought thus can be traced back to Kitabatake and Kusunoki. See! This is the transcendental power that pervades our history! The spirit of Kitabatake and Kusunoki motivated Ansai three hundred years later, Ansai's spirit motivated Yoshida Tōkō more than a hundred years later, who then inspired ... Hashimoto Keigaku to sacrifice himself for his country ...*[84]

Hiraizumi began criticizing the Japanese school education system — that already was highly nationalistic oriented — as lacking the core for character development because "through pure rote learning of periodic data and historical names history loses all of its meaning." Hiraizumi asserted: "Only teaching based on the foundational spirit would ensure ... that every Japanese can awake in his determination and grasp the reason for his existence."[85] In October 1929, the publicist Tokutomi Sohō (1863-1957) organized a seventy years commemoration event for the heroes of the *Ansei* Purges of 1858/1859 when many Imperial loyalists, including Hashimoto and Yoshida, were arrested and executed by the authorities. Hiraizumi spoke at the event about Hashimoto; he was then introduced to Prince Takamatsu, the younger brother of Emperor Hirohito.[86]

1. 3. Being abroad in Europe, 1930-1931

In January 1930 Hiraizumi received the request from the Ministry of Education
(*monbushō*) for a two years study trip to Europe. Such a 'study sojourn abroad'
(*zaigai kenkyū*) was mostly obligatory for any aspiring academic in Japan since
the Meiji period. Before his departure in March, Admiral Arima invited him
to the »Naval War College« (*kaigun daigakkō*) for a speech. In his presentation
he showed the officers in the audience a Japanese sword that a friend had
given him on parting. On the blade was a verse engraved, written by the poet
Tachibana Akemi (1812-1868) from Fukui who had belonged the *kokugaku*
movement:

What is out there?

Besides taking action for the Imperial Land?

—Being in this world![87]

When he left Yokohama on the steamer *Katorimaru*, Hiraizumi wrote in his
cabin an essay about the *'Japanese Spirit'* which Arima had requested from
him as teaching material for the Imperial Navy. Hiraizumi determined the
spirit's essence in the heroic deeds of Yoshida and Hashimoto and brought
the manuscript to the Japanese consulate in Shanghai during the ship's stop
there.[88]

He arrived in Marseille in early May 1930, where he took a train to Germany
and stayed several days each in Göttingen, Nuremberg, Rothenburg and
Munich. In Munich he visited professor Karl Haushofer (1869-1946) who
connected with the Nazi movement through his pioneering research in the

field of *'Geopolitik.'* Haushofer had visited Japan before the First World War and wrote several books about Japan and the Far East between 1921 and 1925. He gave Hiraizumi a recommendation letter for the historian Karl Alexander von Müller (1882-1964), another nationalistic academic that later worked for the Nazi regime.[89]

In Berlin Hiraizumi visited a German high school (»Das Gymnasium zum Grauen Kloster«) led by the nationalist Arnold Reimann (1870-1938) whose educational theory attracted him. Reimann propagated an awakening of the German nation. He saw the purpose of the Treaty of Versailles in the "perpetual disarmament and economic and moral destruction of Germany" and warned repeatedly: "The war is not over yet!" A Japanese friend in Berlin explained to Hiraizumi the *Addresses to the German Nation* by the philosopher Johann Gottlieb Fichte (1762-1814) that had stirred the German national conscience during the Napoleonic Wars.[90]

Hiraizumi spoke in Berlin at »Friedrich Wilhelm University« with the historian Friedrich Meinecke (1862-1954) who focused on early modern German intellectual and cultural history. Meinecke explained to him the topic of his recent lecture titled ›*Geschichte, Staat und Gegenwart*‹ (›*History, the State and the Present*‹), in which he set an Archimedean fixed position—"what we adhere to" ("*woran wir festhalten*")—against the common perception of history as 'constant flowing' (Greek: '*panta rhei*') according to the ancient Greek historian Heraclitus.[91] He gave Hiraizumi his essay ›*Kausalitäten und Werte in der Geschichte*‹ (›*Causalities and Values in History*‹) in which he argued to have detected in the state a spiritual-moral causality that pervades all of history:

To turn the state, in which one lives, into a spiritual and moral entity … this is, next to the imperative to spiritually and morally elevate one's own character, the highest requirement in regard to ethical action—simply because the state is the most effective and most comprehensive of all living communities and because a human being, that strives for perfection, can only breath freely in a state that also pursues perfection.[92]

In October 1930, Hiraizumi travelled through the Balkans to Greece and Italy where he visited Croce in Naples. He came to Paris and bought books about the French Revolution, in which he read how its three guiding principles had originated differently: *liberté* was evoked in 1789, *égalité* was proclaimed in 1792 and *fraternité* was added in 1848. He sought verification for his 'discovery' and went to ask French historians. The Marxist professor Albert Mathiez (1874-1932), who saw the French Revolution as a class conflict and lauded the Jacobin Maximilien de Robespierre (1758-1794), agreed with Hiraizumi and encouraged him to continue his research. Hiraizumi began to question the 'moral weight' of the French Revolution as the centerpiece of modern European history. He talked with the novelist Paul Bourget (1852-1935) who wrote for a traditional audience of Catholics and Monarchists. Bourget introduced to him other texts written by French conservatives and royalists.[93]

Hiraizumi arrived in England in April 1931 and met the poet and author Edmund Blunden (1896-1974) who had taught English literature at Tōkyō Imperial University from 1924 until 1927. Blunden gave him six books about the French Revolution including a volume of the conservative philosopher Edmund Burke (1729-1797) who had argued strongly against the French Revolution during its time. While Hiraizumi immersed himself in Burke's writings in London, he began sensing that his country, Japan, was on the verge of an imminent crisis for which it was not 'spiritually' prepared. He requested at the Japanese embassy his return ahead of schedule and came back to Japan via the United States.[94]

Arima Ryōkitsu

Matsudaira Yoshitami

Prince Chichibu

Kido Kōichi

2. 'Times of National Emergency', the 1930s

Hiraizumi was back in Tōkyō in July 1931 to resume his work at the university.[95] Two months later, on September 18th, the Japanese *Guandong-Army (Kantōgun)* staged the 'Manchurian Incident' by detonating an explosion at the *South Manchuria Railway* line and used it as a pretext for occupying the vast regions of Manchuria without consulting the Japanese government. This sudden development confirmed Hiraizumi's sense of foreboding that he'd felt for a year. The takeover of Manchuria provoked diplomatic friction with the Western Powers and the League of Nations, which in turn led in Japan to a mood of defiance and the perception that a 'time of emergency' (*hijōji*) has arrived.

On October 17th 1931 Hiraizumi went to visit Admiral Katō Kanji (Katō Hiroharu, 1870-1939) who also was from Fukui and led the *Keigakukai* society since Hatta's death in January 1930. Katō represented the 'Fleet faction' (*kantaiha*) in the Navy that had formed in opposition to the armament reductions in accordance with the *London Naval Treaty* that the Japanese government had signed a year before. Whilst talking, Katō received a telephone call about the arrest of several Army staff officers who supposedly prepared a *coup d'état*. This 'Brocade Banner Revolution' (*kinki kakumei*)—also called the 'October Incident' (*jūgatsu jiken*)—was kept secret from the public but details spread among the elites. It was the second *coup* attempt by military men and right-wing affiliates after the similar 'March Incident' (*sangatsu jiken*) of that same year. The event was the topic of discussion during a *Fukui Club* gathering in the residence of Matsudaira Yoshitami on 21st October 1931, when Hiraizumi got acquainted with Admiral Okada Keisuke (1868-1952), the *Fukuikai*'s new chairman—he too was from Fukui. A few weeks later, Admiral

Arima—he just had become the main priest at the Meiji-Shrine (*Meiji jingū*) in Tōkyō—called Hiraizumi to the *Yūshūkai* to report on his trip to Europe.[96]

In January 1932, Ichiki Kitokurō (1867-1944), the Imperial Household Minister (*kunai daijin*), asked the rector of Tōkyō Imperial University Onozuka Kiheiji (1871-1944) to select a professor to be a private teacher for Prince Chichibu, the Emperor's sibling who was next in line of throne succession. Prince Chichibu had graduated from the »Army War College« (*rikugun daigakkō*) in the fall of 1931 and currently served as a Captain in the »First Infantry Division« (*dai'ichi shidan*). Onozuka asked Hiraizumi to accept the honor. From March 1932 until July 1933 Hiraizumi taught Chichibu and his wife Setsuko every Wednesday evening the "history of politics in Japan", by which he meant "the political principle of Imperial rule in Japan since its foundation."[97]

Chichibu had ties to military reform circles that sought to solve the socio-political crisis in Japan during the Great Depression through a *coup* to initiate wide ranging reforms under the banner of a 'Shōwa Restoration.' Since his time at the Army Academy in 1922, he was acquainted with Nishida Mitsugi (1901-1937), the companion of the right-wing ideologue Kita Ikki, whose *Outline Plan for the Reorganization of Japan* was considered to be the blueprint for fundamental reforms in state and society. Chichibu sympathized with the 'Cherry Blossom Society' (*Sakurakai*) that planned the *March Incident* and he was possibly involved in the *Brocade Banner Revolution* too.[98] Hiraizumi's role seemed to have been to advise the prince of his duties as the possible heir to the throne.

As Japanese society became more polarized during the economic depression, the Imperial universities saw an increase in 'Marxist incidents.' This prompted Hiraizumi in November 1931 to form a right-wing student group—the 'Society of Red Light' (*Shukōkai*)—modeled after the 'Society of Seven Lives' (*Shichiseisha*) that Uesugi had created in 1925 to counter left-wing tendencies but that didn't have any impact in its days.[99] On 11th February 1932, the *Shukōkai* proclaimed its manifesto:

- *We firmly believe in Emperor centrism.*
- *We want to polish our characters on the basis of the Imperial Way.*

- *We want to promote the traditions of learning in frugality and determination.*
- *We want to build up Japan according to its Foundational Spirit.*
- *We promise to spread the Spirit of Greater Japan to the whole world.*[100]

On the same day (February 11th: Imperial Japan's national 'Foundation Day' *kigensetsu* when Emperor Jinmu was said to have ascended the throne), Ōkawa, who previously had joined the *Brocade Banner Revolution*, proclaimed a new movement called the '*Jinmu* Society' (*Jinmukai*) to create a "Japanese reform avant-garde" that would affect the upcoming parliamentary elections on February 20th 1932 through street agitation and to bring 'patriotic candidates' into office who would tackle the economic crisis with broad support from the population. His plan failed and right-wing groups gained almost no seats in the election. Hiraizumi met Ōkawa in these days, who asked him to publish an article in his journal *Gekkan Nihon*.[101]

Ōkawa continued his activism and eventually handed several Browning pistols to the naval lieutenants who then tried to stage a *coup d'état* on May 15th 1932 and shot prime minister Inukai Tsuyoshi (1855-1932) in his office. The 'May-15 Incident' (*goichigo jiken*), which in its initial plan targeted several politicians, shook the fragile status quo, as a contemporary commentator wrote:

> *The decay of the political parties had already started during the last days of the Wakatsuki Cabinet ... The sound of the mortal shot aimed at Inukai at his official residence ... made Japanese society feel more keenly than ever the pressure of the "emergency period" that was fast overcoming it.*[102]

Hiraizumi continued his letter correspondence with Ōkawa who was arrested for his involvement in the *May-15* plot.[103] But he clearly rejected any kind of upheaval—from the left or right—and formulated arguments against it.[104] The Ministry of Education called on him to participate in setting up the »People's Spiritual Culture Research Institute« (*kokumin seishin bunka kenkyūjo*) with the aim to thwart left-wing tendencies and "strengthen the youths' consciousness towards the Imperial Land." Conservative professors were assigned to speak at tertiary schools and over the spring and summer of 1932. Hiraizumi visited several high and technical schools where he spoke against the 'validity' of a revolution in Japan.[105]

In his speeches he dismissed the 'social contract' idea of Jean-Jacques Rousseau (1712-1778) as well as the Confucian concept of 'Mandate Change' (jp. *kakumei*, chin. *geming*) by which the Chinese philosopher Mencius (c. 372-289 BC) had justified violent dynastic changes in ancient China. Hiraizumi declared both formulae to be 'inadmissible' in Japan because—by his reasoning—the unbroken Imperial line made Japan into a country with a 'true history' that excludes any revolution, meaning in a nation with a *true history* a revolution simply can't occur as it is prevented by its *National spirit*, while on the other side, in a land, where a revolution had taken place, its *lineage*, *tradition* and *spirit* are destroyed and its 'historical substance' and 'true history' are therefore dead. In Japan, as Hiraizumi repeatedly stressed, the Emperor is solely in charge of political 'renewal' (*ishin*): "Renewal is the principle-based antipode to a revolution."[106]

He repeated Yamazaki's critique of the Confucians' acceptance of dynastic change in China, which began with the brutal overthrow of the Shang dynasty by the Zhou in 1046 BC while claiming a continuation in rites and order that laid out the procedures for all following acts of power seizure. In his lectures *Kōyūsō furoku* (1692) Yamazaki dismissed the *Mandate Change* notion as a mere condonation for usurpation and gave credence only to the Han Emperor Guangwu who rebuilt his own dynasty after defeating the usurper Wang Mang in AD 25. In moral contrast to China, Yamazaki saw Japan's Imperial house as the embodiment of an ideal and benign rulership continuation, so he declared unconditional allegiance (*chū*) to the throne—as exemplified best by Kusunoki—to be every subject's highest duty (*gi*) in the realm.[107]

Arima asked Hiraizumi to organize a memorial event for the 250th anniversary of Yamazaki's death. With the support of rector Onozuka and the nationalist philosopher Inoue Tetsujirō (1856-1944), Hiraizumi directed the 'Ansai festival' at Tōkyō Imperial University on 23rd of October 1932 which was honored by Prince Takamatsu's attendance.[108] Hiraizumi wrote the companion book *Ansai sensei to Nihon seishin* (»Master Ansai and the Japanese Spirit«), in which he described the genealogy of the *spirit of self-sacrifice* for the Imperial cause that, according to him, had originated with Yamazaki's thinking. Hiraizumi ignored the different opinions among Yamazaki's followers[109] and declared:

> *To clarify the lofty principle that [the Emperor] is the ruler over the subjects and to feel it within one's own body, [it must be understood that] this spirit began with Master Ansai, then flowed into his school of thought and thus was transmitted to the following generations. Because of this spirit, Asami Keisai recognized the primacy of loyalty towards Emperor and towards patriotism, and because of this spirit Wakabayashi Kyōsai began to honor Kusunoki. ... Over time, this spirit became brighter when ... [at the end of the Tokugawa era] Takenouchi Shikibu [died on his way into exile], when Yamagata Daini and Fujii Naoaki were executed, when Takayama Hikokurō cut his stomach wide open and was followed in the same manner by Karasaki Hitachinosuke, when Umeda Unpin died in prison because he had propagated this highest principle, and when Hashimoto Keigaku ... was put to death. Other men too ... fought for the Emperor until finally the Meiji Restoration received wider public support (yokusan).*

> *Of course, we must also recognize many other thinkers who contributed their parts in elucidating the kokutai and honoring the Emperor, but the steadfast propagation of the lofty principle, that there is [the Emperor as] a ruler over his subjects, as a criticism of their time, and the personal [consequences] when one teacher after another fell [being prosecuted by the Shogunate], just to be followed up by another teacher, and in this manner for over more than two centuries hundreds of men rose up everywhere in support of the Emperor, this process took place solely and only in the Kimon school.[110]*

The *Ansai festival* was the first large celebration of a premodern Japanese school of thought at Tōkyō Imperial University after decades of focusing on Western traditions which subsequently led to revaluations of the *Kimon* thinkers in the academic field. [111] Hiraizumi used his growing scholarly standing to criticize those historians who saw the Ashikaga backed *Northern*

Court in the fourteenth century as legitimate because of an overall acceptance of Godaigo's *Southern Line*, was the precondition for the *spiritual genealogy* that Hiraizumi constructed to advocate the highest duty towards the state. He referred to the writings of his academic mentor professor Kuroita during the *Southern-Northern Court Debate* in 1911, who had emphasized the topic's significance for national education as Lisa Yoshikawa noted: "Unless Go Daigo's legitimacy was established, pupils might doubt his supporter Kusunoki Masashige and his value as a loyal subject."[112]

Hiraizumi's new book *Kokushigaku no kotsuzui* (»The Mark of our National Historiography«), a collection of his recent articles, came out in September 1932.[113] He focused now on the *Jinnō shōtōki* as the Imperial state's 'historical core document' and demanded to base the entire school education system on it. He published the old handwritten *Jinnō shōtōki* version that belonged to his ancestral shrine[114] and he edited a *Jinnō shōtōki* textbook for the Ministry of Education to be used in the high school curriculum.[115] Oddly enough, Hiraizumi was accused of *lèse-majesté* for one commentary section in this book but the evolving scandal was put to an end by Hiranuma Kiichirō (1867-1952) who controlled the Justice Department and had strong leverage over right-wing groups.[116] Hiraizumi also changed the travel destinations for the annual seminar trips. In the fall of 1932, he went with the first semester group to Mito and Tsukuba in Ibaraki Prefecture, where Kitabatake had written the *Jinnō shōtōki* whilst under siege by Ashikaga allies. With the second semester group he visited the places of the *Southern Court* in the Kansai area.[117]

2. 1. Gaining public weight

Admiral Arima introduced Hiraizumi to Army Minister Araki Sadao (1877-1966), the outspoken Lt. General who advocated the 'Imperial Way' (*kōdō*) to overcome the nation's problems through moral leadership of the military. Araki arranged for him to make a presentation before Emperor Hirohito on December 5th 1932. Hiraizumi chose his preferred topic: "The historical achievement of Kusunoki Masashige." The court official Kido Kōichi noted in his diary: "I listened intently how Masashige sacrificed his whole family for the highest principle during Godaigo's *Kenmu* renewal ... and how he was thoroughly loyal without any regrets." But Hirohito was not impressed and Makino Nobuaki (1861-1949), the Lord Keeper of the Privy Seal (*naidaijin*), agreed. Yuasa Kurahei (1874-1940), who three months later would become Minister of the Imperial Household, wrote: "His Majesty too was of the opinion that [Hiraizumi] trivialized things. ... His simple glorification of the *Kenmu* Restoration was not particularly interesting for his Majesty."[118]

Hiraizumi wasn't invited to speak in front of Hirohito again but his reputation grew because of this one time 'call before His Majesty' and his name gained traction as he later said.[119] High-ranking men from politics, military and bureaucracy reached out to him. He was contacted by Major General Obata Toshirō (1885-1947) from the General Staff, a close associate of Araki in the 'Imperial Way Faction' (*kōdōha*) of the Army. Obata invited him to the founding assembly of the 'Greater Asia Society' (*Dai'ajia kyōkai*) on 26th of January 1933 where he was introduced to Prince Konoe Fumimaro. Konoe began to receive him privately. Kido wrote in his diary about his meeting with Konoe and Hiraizumi on 7th of February 1933:

At six o'clock I had dinner with Prince Konoe and Dr. Hiraizumi at the Peers' Club (kazoku kaikan). *Dr. Hiraizumi informed us about the recent communist trends at the universities. According to him, communism is spreading everywhere, a frightening development indeed. Dr. Hiraizumi believes that such advances could lead to the [eventual] failure of the great Meiji Restoration exactly as it did during the Kenmu Renewal, which would be irresponsible. He stresses that the essential core of a Shōwa Renovation* (Shōwa ishin) *must be Personal Imperial Rule* (tennō shinsei). *A lot of what he is saying earns attention.*[120]

With "communist trends at the universities" Hiraizumi presumedly also meant the Marxist group around Hani that had founded the 'Historical Science Society' (*rekishigaku kenkyūkai*) at Tōkyō Imperial University in December 1932.[121] In an attempt to appeal to a left-wing audience, Hiraizumi wrote an article for the journal *Kaizō* (»Reconstruction«) that mainly printed socialist and socially related content, in which he tried to rebrand Hashimoto as a societal reformer:

A time of crisis requires extremely prudent decisions and such decisions require extraordinary personalities. Because it's hard to solve all the conflicts … and problems during the current times of emergency, the people are waiting for special protagonists to appear. Let us therefore look at previous critical times, especially the Taika Reforms, the Kenmu Renewal and the Meiji Restoration, and let us be reminded of the heroes from those ages who mastered the challenges of their times by giving their lives for it. The time when the Bakufu ended and Meiji began … is still in the people's memories and the protagonists are well known. The commemoration of these heroes is still popular today but among their sheer numbers Yoshida Shōin from Chōshū and Hashimoto Keigaku from Echizen stand out distinctively.[122]

On request from »Hokkaidō Imperial University« (*Hokkaidō teikoku daigaku*) he went to Sapporo in March 1933 and gave three lectures before the gathered faculties to address the growth of socialist ideas among students. He presented (1) a philosophical framework by merging professor Meinecke's theory of the

Causalities and Values in History with Japan's loyalist thought tradition. (2) He then stressed the importance of Fichte's writings for uniting the German nation in the nineteenth century. (3) Finally, he countered Heraclitus' dictum that 'everything flows' *(panta rhei*; jp. *banbutsu ruten)* with — in his words — the 'unchanging way' *(fueki no michi)* of the values of 'loyalty and filiality' *(chūkō)* as the highest moral norm that was best expressed in the spirit of the *shishi* loyalists whose "heroic deeds brought about the Meiji Restoration."[123]

Because of Hiraizumi's unwillingness to question the *status quo* of elite politics, he came to oppose the patriotic groups who envisioned socio-political changes through a *Shōwa Restoration* to resolve the material rift in society that had worsened sharply during the Depression. Hiraizumi vaguely upheld the ideal of 'Personal Imperial Rule' *(tennō shinsei)* — that formed the core of a *Shōwa Restoration* for many right-wing reformers — but he didn't advocate any specific reforms as that would have challenged the existing power structure that infuriated many young patriots as well as the Marxists. Major General Shibuya Inohiko (1881-1935) called Hiraizumi to the Army Academy explicitly for the purpose of reminding the cadets of their duty to obey their superiors because some them still sympathized with the *May 1932 Revolt*. This assigned role as a 'tranquillizer', as Hiraizumi later called it, provoked repulsion by radicalized officers and led to an incident at the »Toyama Army Academy« *(rikugun Toyama gakkō)* on March 17th 1933 when Hiraizumi was physically threatened by a lieutenant with a drawn Japanese sword.[124]

In April 1933 Hiraizumi set up a private tutoring facility named the »Fresh Green Academy« *(Seiseijuku)* near his house in Akebono Tōkyō to train selected students and military men in the principle of loyalty. He envisioned the *Seiseijuku* to be a place of patriotic learning that would shape future leaders just like the romanticized *Shōka sonjuku* academy (»The Village School under the Pine Trees«) in Hagi city, the capital of former Chōshū Domain (now Yamaguchi Prefecture), where Yoshida Shōin had instructed high-minded men like Takasugi Shinsaku (1839-1867), Itō Hirobumi (1841-1909) and Yamagata Aritomo (1838-1922) — the heroes who had then toppled the Tokugawa system and initiated the Meiji Restoration. Hiraizumi took the name *Fresh Green Academy* (also translated as »Green Green Academy«) from a poem of the Chinese scholar and politician Xie Fangde (1226-1289) who, when captured by the Mongols, refused to give up his allegiance to the defeated Southern Song Empire (960-1279). When he was to be brought to the Mongols' capital of Khanbaliq (Beijing) to eventually die there, Xie advised his family and friends with the following verse to be forever loyal to the Song:

The conifers in the snow

Become greener and greener.

Those whose have the eternal principles rooted in them,

All follow this path.[125]

Hiraizumi later explained this:

> *This means to walk the path, which must be followed, without any deviation and to protect steadfastly the principle, that must be saved, no matter what difficulties one encounters and what trouble one might face. It's the will to anticipate a looming crisis for the nation and to forge an ironlike determination through the respect towards the loyalty of those men from the past.*[126]

On Major General Obata's recommendation, Hiraizumi travelled to the newly created Japanese puppet state Manchukuo (*Manshūkoku*) during the spring of 1933, where he spoke at *Guandong*-Army's headquarters and was received by regent Pu Yi (1906-1967) who was declared Emperor of Manchukuo one year later. Over the summer of 1933, Hiraizumi made another lecture tour to all together 43 schools throughout Japan on the request of the Education Ministry. In his visits he emphasized the primacy of the Imperial initiative in the case of political reform. He juxtaposed this superior Japanese principle of 'renewal' (*ishin*) to the Chinese and Western way of 'revolution' (*kakumei*) that only destroys the historical-spiritual continuance of a nation. [127] In a presentation at the *People's Spiritual Culture Research Institute* he declared:

> *Yamazaki Ansai's and Asami Keisai's thoughts on the [Confucian concept of] Mandate Change were clear. Keisai was succeeded by Wakabayashi Kyōsai who vigorously taught the principle of ruler and subject, and who revered as the ideal character; nobody other than General Kusunoki. ... This shows that no matter how one may think about a revolution in normal times, in a time of crisis we give our*

46

lives and protect the Imperial mission, and by doing so we follow the [ancient] gods'

commandment that the Empire will last for eternity (tenjō mukyū no shinchoku).

History and revolution contradict each other. They don't fit together because

history only becomes history when it's pervaded by a flawless spirit. It's therefore

evident that history dies when that spirit is interrupted or terminated, that's exactly

what a revolution causes.[128]

Japan's withdrawal from the League of Nations on March 27th 1933, the expansion of its military operations in Northern China and the patriotic conversion (*tenkō*) of several high-profile Japanese communists in the summer of 1933 led to a nationwide wave of nationalism. Hiraizumi proclaimed an awakening of Asia through the Japanese spirit:

To bring the world onto its right path, Asia must become Asia, and for this Japan

must first become Japan. To accomplish this, Japan's baseless copying of foreign

civilizations must end and the real Japanese spirit must return. Hence the bushidō

spirit must ... awaken in us again.[129]

This text ›*Bushidō no fukkatsu*‹ (›The revival of the Warrior's Creed‹) became the lead essay for his new book with the same title.[130] Hiraizumi also took part in the edition of the »Seminar Series on the Japanese Spirit« (*Nippon seishin kōza*), a vast collection of articles dwelling on Japanese nationalism written by scholars, intellectuals, military men and politicians that spanned up to twelve volumes in 1935. Hiraizumi penned the prefatory essay titled ›*Bushidō no shinzui*‹ (›The marrow of the Warrior's Creed‹) for the first volume that came out in the fall 1933:

The flower mostly beloved by the Japanese is the cherry blossom. ... The cherry

blossom must be called the symbol of the Japanese spirit. ... To see the cherry

blossom suddenly fall ... and to realize that we might die for the Emperor at any

given day in such purity, ... this cherry blossom is the seriousness and depth in the

Japanese spirit because it corresponds with the Warrior's Way.[131]

On the 23rd December 1933, Akihito, the male successor to the throne (the later *Heisei Emperor* from 1990 to 2019) was born. Prince Konoe asked Hiraizumi to write his congratulatory speech which Konoe read on radio as chairman of the House of Peers (*kizoku'in*).[132] In January 1934, Hiraizumi held a lecture tour at the naval bases Yokosuka, Sasebo and Kure, the Navy Academy in Etajima (Hiroshima), the »Navy Engineering College« (*kaigun kikan gakkō*) in Maizuru (Kyōto Prefecture) and finally the Naval War College in Tōkyō at the end of the month, followed by eight more speeches there over the year, in which he glorified the *Warrior's Creed* and obedience to the throne as the *spirit* of the Japanese people.[133] The style of his presentations caused one Naval officer to write a complaint because he saw no value in Hiraizumi's one-sided and oversimplifying praise of the 'loyal vassals' (*chūshin*) while debasing the 'traitors' (*gyakushin*) in Japanese history.[134] The Army was more appreciative of his message. Obata called him to address the »First Guard Infantry Regiment« (*Konoe hohei dai'ichi rentai*) in December 1933. During a speech at the Army Academy on April 16th 1934, Hiraizumi held up a Japanese sword and exclaimed:

Army! Listen! ... This sword was crafted ... in 1862 and can cut every opponent into two halves. ... Army! Be so sharp and splendid like this sword! During the thirty years of peace since the war against Russia [1904-1905] our country has become soft and idle and there isn't a trace of the spirit of courage and service for the nation anymore. One day, this country will be in danger. ... Look at this sword! The engraved verse says: "Where the mountains split and where the seas dry up, even in such a world I will never betray the ruler." As everybody knows, so did the third Kamakura-Shōgun Minamoto Sanetomo swear with this verse absolute obedience to Emperor Gotoba, no matter what happens. This is the right thing to do! Only with the spirit of perfect loyalty, military strength becomes useful. ... The might of our Imperial Army can only be activated and applied through Imperial Order and by no means can it operate independently. ... Army! Show Your might in loyalty and act out on an Imperial order![135]

After the presentation, Major General Tōjō Hideki introduced himself to Hiraizumi. A few days later, Tōjō visited him at his home with the request to prepare a whole lecture series for one year at the Army Academy, for which Hiraizumi should select the teachers and materials. Obata, who had become the head of the Army War College in March 1934, called Hiraizumi to several 'special lectures' over the summer and autumn. In June Hiraizumi conducted a three-day-seminar for reserve units of the »Eleventh Infantry Division« (*dai jūichi shidan*) in Zentsūji (Kagawa Prefecture).[136]

On 8 July 1934 Admiral Okada received the Imperial order to form a new government. On that same evening, Hiraizumi was invited together with Matsudaira and the other *Fukui Club* members to the Prime Minister's residence. Admiral Katō didn't attend because of his quarrel with Okada, who together with Vice Admiral Yonai Mitsumasa (1880-1948) represented the Navy's 'Treaty Faction' (*keiyakuha*) that supported the arms limitations of the *London Naval Conference*. Hiraizumi shared Katō's views regarding the necessity of an armaments program but he persuaded him in the following months to cooperate with the Okada cabinet.[137] Matsudaira rose to 'Grand Master of Ceremonies' (*shikibu chōkan*) in the *Imperial Household Ministry* in July 1934. He asked Hiraizumi to help his son Nagayoshi to prepare for the Naval Academy's entrance exam. Nagayoshi then lived for about a year in Hiraizumi's house together with his wife and three sons. Ultimately, he failed the exam and entered the Navy Engineering College in Maizuru in 1935.[138]

2. 2. The Kenmu Restoration's 600th anniversary

In 1934 the promulgation of the *Kenmu Restoration* marked its sixth centennial. After his allies had destroyed the Kamakura Shogunate in 1333, Emperor Godaigo proclaimed the era *Kenmu* at the start of the new year on 13 March 1334 (according to the Lunar Calendar), by which the Imperial court's political power would be restored after 150 years since the end of the Heian period. In December 1933, a 'Kenmu Restoration 600th Anniversary Remembrance Committee' (*Kenmu no chūkō roppyakunen kinenkai*) was set up with Arima as chairman and Prince Chichibu as nominal president to prepare for a wide range of events in Tōkyō, Ōsaka and Kyōto, where Hiraizumi and Kuroita made a series of speeches that included a historical ceremony in the Yoyogi Youth Hall (*Nihon seinenkan*) next to the Meiji Shrine.[139] Professor Yoshikawa described these activities:

For the Kenmu centennial, Kuroita and Matsudaira [Yorinaga] promoted the events and recruited over ten organizations to support their efforts. Participating groups included the city of Tokyo, the Shrine Association, the proto-Great Japanese Youth Organization, the Veteran's Association, naval associations, and the National Education Association. Kuroita also acted as a trustee of the celebration committee and contributed an article to the commemoration booklet that repeated the gist of his earlier writings on the emperor.

The festivities included a lecture series in Tokyo and other regions, ceremonies for the imperial loyalists, related historic sites tours, dispatching of representatives to all shrines related to the Restoration, and exhibits at the Osaka Mitsukoshi department store and the Osaka castle. Many of these events were modeled on the successful Shōtoku [Taishi] celebration over a decade earlier. ... Asahi ran a column about the Kenmu centennial to attract readers. Kuroita contributed his nine-part series in this forum. The Yoshino Shrine held a formal commemorative event at its precinct, which provided an opportunity for Kuroita to train Hiraizumi Kiyoshi as his successor for these endeavors.[140]

Hiraizumi and his assistants provided the texts for the 359-pages book *Kenmu no chūkō* that the *Remembrance Committee* issued.[141] He also published his own book, *Kenmu no chūkō no hongi* (»The *Kenmu* Renewal's Core Principle«), in which he presented an Emperor-centric view of Japanese history by combining the historical reform endeavors initiated by the Court — the *Taika Reforms* in the 7th century, the *Kenmu-* and the *Meiji Restoration* — into a three-step progression scheme: (1) After the gods bestowed Emperor Jinmu with the mandate to create the Japanese nation, "this great ideal of the ancient times was finally realized with the *Taika* edicts" in the Asuka period (538-710) that unified the realm under the Emperor's authority based on the model of the Tang dynasty. (2) After the Kamakura *Bakufu*'s "illegitimate reign ... that stood in contradiction to the *kokutai*," Godaigo reestablished "the natural order of Imperial rule, ... the true Japan," but he faced betrayal by Ashikaga Takauji who deposed him and set up another Shogunate. (3) Finally, the glorious *Meiji Restoration* created the modern state "in accordance with the great ideal of the past."[142]

The *Kenmu* era, so Hiraizumi, constituted therefore the "central axis in the history of Japan" (*Nihonshi no chūjiku*), "its most eminent event before the modern age" for it placed the seed of the *spirit of Imperial loyalism* that later enabled the Meiji Restoration to occur. But, he warned, it also casts its shadow on the current times as a harbinger for a looming existential crisis because the nation became 'careless' since the Taishō years (1912-1926) and the state might soon face a similar fate as the *Kenmu* Restoration. This crisis could only be averted by a vigorous 'Renewal of Japan' (*Nihon chūkō*) through collective reflection and a new emphasis on the *spirit of self-sacrifice* by abandoning all 'un-Japanese thinking' that had intruded into society from foreign countries during the past decades:[143]

The reason for the failure of the Kenmu Restoration is therefore clear. Because many men had forgotten the higher principle (gi) *and followed their self-interest* (ri). *The fair-minded politics of the Imperial Court didn't reach them anymore and they were enticed by Ashikaga Takauji, the master of intrigue; they assembled under his banner … and the wide-reaching Imperial reform project crumbled. … Our forefathers didn't only not support* (yokusan) *the Imperial endeavor, but they also carry the guilt … in which the following six hundred years the lofty mandate was reviled. The history of the Kenmu Restoration must be read with tears of remorse! And it shouldn't be misunderstood as a mere historical or nostalgic tale! The problems of the Kenmu era are the same as today! How about the current discrepancy between high principle and self-interest? How many people today ignore our history, dismiss the* kokutai *by ideologically meandering around, don't see the high principle or pursue perfidious or haughty aims? And how many, on the other side, resist these trends, search for the true way, know their standing as real Japanese, serve the Emperor … and wish to defend the higher principle with their death? The problem wasn't 'six hundred years ago!' It's here and today directly among us 'six hundred years since then!'*[144]

In his university lecture about the Japanese Middle Ages (*chūsei kōgi*) he now primarily talked about the French Revolution, dismissing it as the "principal mistake of the modern times" that instigated the destruction of the traditions:

Those who want to revive Japan's true tradition must abandon the superstitious belief in the French Revolution, that the Meiji and Taishō generations grappled with, and must free themselves from its strong influence. … The French Revolution now goes back 150 years, its horrors have faded from the public view and there isn't much interest in it anymore. However, the French Revolution initiated the betrayal against the traditions and called for upheaval, not only in France but all over the world. That's why it resembles the Soviet Union. No, it's exactly like the USSR which continues its intent and legacy! Because Lenin … got his ideas from … Marx who got his revolutionary zeal from the French Revolution. … Luckily, our forefathers saved us from a revolution [in Japan]. But today the trickling in of revolutionary thinking is occurring everywhere. Tackling the dismissal of the past and the aversion against our forefathers' history, we must take ... the French Revolution's influence very seriously.[145]

In 1934, the Ishikawa Prefecture Police Department printed a speech that he had given at the invitation of Tomita Kenji (1897-1977), a higher official who took part in his *Seiseijuku* academy sessions. This booklet with the title »Loyalty and Principle« (*Chū to gi*) gave a synopsis of Hiraizumi's ideology: The 'higher loyalty' towards Emperor and state—meaning protection of the monarchy at all costs—supersedes and transcends all kind of 'lower loyalties' that the social order demands from the individual.[146] Hiraizumi detailed this theme in ten special lectures at the Army War College over the spring of 1935, followed by similar courses for middle ranking officers at the Army Academy.[147] He claimed that the *kokutai*'s continuation throughout history "has only been possible because of the undeterred actions by Imperial loyalists imbued with the distinct spirit who sacrificed their own lives for the higher cause in times of crisis." He continued:

In no way should our history be perceived in an optimistic way. People often refer with pride to "the glory of our kokutai.*" However, [the* kokutai*] was always protected with the blood of our wise predecessors* (sentetsu) *and by no means simply passed down to us [naturally]. ... Of course, the* kokutai *originated with our Heavenly Forefathers ... but it was honorably handed to us because wise men had given their lives for it in confronting the vacuous thinking [of their times] and singularly opposing a vast majority [of wrong-thinkers].*[148]

In March of 1935 Hiraizumi became the academic successor for the retiring Kuroita as head of the 'Second Professorial Chair for Japanese History' (*kokushi daini kōza*) at Tōkyō Imperial University Simultaneously he took over as chairman of the 'Historical Society of Japan' (*shigakkai*) that published the leading academic journal *Shigaku zasshi*.[149] After his promotion to full professor, a large series of events to commemorate General Kusunoki was held all over the Japanese Empire. Hiraizumi invited Kuroita, one of the main supervising organizers, to a '600 Years Kusunoki Memorial' (*Dainankō roppyakunen taisai*) at his home shrine in Fukui from 19 to 22 May 1935. This event at the *Hakusan* Shrine, to which Matsudaira Yoshitami and Admiral Katō also came, was held under the motto: "Here before [Kusunoki's] tomb, far away from the public in this time of emergency, ... we must clarify the high principle of ruler and subject and intensify the great way of loyalty and filialty."[150] Hiraizumi and Kuroita then overviewed the 'Kusunoki Warriors Parade' (*Nankō musha gyōretsu*) in Kōbe (24-26 May), celebrating Kusunoki's historical meeting with Godaigo.[151] The *Taiheiki* wrote about this episode that occurred in the spring of 1333, from where the Emperor and his Army marched on Kyōto to proclaim the Imperial government:

Kusunoki Tamon Masashige of the Middle Palace Guards came to meet [the Emperor] with seven thousand horsemen. He was a most impressive figure. His Majesty raised the blinds [of his palanquin] high and, having summoned Masashige to approach, addressed him gratefully: "The rapid triumph of our Great Cause is due entirely to your loyal fighting." Masashige made obeisance and modestly declined the Emperor's honour: "Were it not for Your Majesty's wise governance of the realm and his godlike skill in quelling disorder, how could the feeble schemes of this poor servant have enabled us to break through so mighty an enemy?"[152]

Professor Yoshikawa summarized the Kusunoki celebrations in 1935:

The events surrounding the Kusunoki Masashige centennial were larger than the Kenmu celebration. They included rituals conducted concurrently at temples and shrines related to Masashige, and exhibits hosted by Asahi, among others, as well as by the city of Kōbe—home to the Minatogawa Shrine honoring Masashige. Commemorative postal stamps were issued, and nationwide moral commemoration ceremonies held. The festivities at the Minatogawa Shrine gathered hundreds of schoolteachers and youth association representatives, who pledged to spread Masashige's imperial loyalist spirit.[153]

Hiraizumi presided over a Kusunoki event at the university in mid-June 1935, in his words "a truly magnificent and solemn celebration in the Law Department's lecture hall and voluntarily attended by students from all faculties."[154] In July, he spoke about Kusunoki at »Kasumigaura Naval Air Base« (*Kasumigaura kaigun kōkutai*) near Mito city. In late July, he travelled to Korea for the 25-years-anniversary of its annexation by Japan and gave speeches about the *Japanese Spirit* before the authorities in Seoul and Incheon. He also made three radio presentations about the Imperial tombs from the *Jōkyū* era as part of an NHK series in cooperation with the Ministry of the Imperial Household.[155]

On November 4th 1935, he attended a ceremony in the Tennōji park in Ōsaka, where a local initiative from the Ikazuri Shrine (*Ikazuri jinja*) erected a stone tablet to honor the loyalist Sakura Azumao (1811-1860). Hiraizumi spoke about Sakura who had entered a Buddhist monastery at the age of nine but left it after reading *Mito* and *kokugaku* treatises to follow the *kokugaku* ideologue Hirata Atsutane (1776-1843). Sakura became a Shintō priest at the Ikazuri Shrine and began travelling through the country to praise the Imperial myths, until he was arrested in connection with the murder of the Shogunate Elder Ii Naosuke (1815-1860) and died in prison from a hunger strike with the following words attributed to him: "I won't eat the Tokugawa's millet!" Hiraizumi glorified him as a 'true Japanese' whose self-chosen name Sakura ('Cherry blossom') "is seen from time immemorial as a symbol of the Japanese spirit to die at any moment in loyalty to the ruler":

The true Japanese tradition ignited a glistening light with Master Sakura. However, Master Sakura was thanked only in part for it. Only in part, because his example of the Imperial subject's way was soon forgotten and the light of our tradition, that he had shown, became weak again. We must clarify the way and allow the light to shine once more. By doing so we show our true gratitude to Master Sakura. When we Japanese all possess his spirit and return to our tradition, in other words, when we become true Japanese, then we can gain ... spiritual unity for the first time. Once we form a collective body that thinks in unison, ... nothing can threaten us from the outside.[156]

Over the course of 1935, right-wing hardliners waged a furious campaign against professor Minobe Tatsukichi (1873-1948), whose teachings constituted the main academic position in Constitutional Law (*kenpōgaku*) since the onset of the Taishō period. Back in 1912, Uesugi unsuccessfully had attacked Minobe's 'Western theory'—which was based on German state law—as violating the '*kokutai* principle' because Minobe placed the Emperor as an 'organ of the state' (*kokka kikan*) into the framework of the Meiji Constitution and limited his prerogatives, while Uesugi elevated him above the constitution without any restrictions by law. Uesugi propagated his views on the Emperor's absolute and unlimited authority—called 'Tennō Sovereignty Theory' (*tennō shuken setsu*)—throughout the parliamentarian phase of the 1920s until he died in 1929 sick in despair that his *kokutai*-based state formula couldn't take a hold in the universities.[157]

With the mood in the country having shifted to the right during the recent years, the attacks against Minobe resumed in February 1935 in the House of Peers with a speech by Lt. General Kikuchi Takeo (1875-1955) and waged for months until the concerted efforts to discredit the 'Tennō Organ Theory' (*tennō kikan setsu*) forced Minobe to resign from the House of Peers on 18 September and put sufficient pressure on the Okada government to issue two successive statements by which Minobe's state interpretation was banned from academia and the *kokutai* state dogma being reinforced.[158] The second »Statement to clarify the *kokutai*« (*kokutai meichō seimei*) on 15th October 1935 read:

> *In our country, the subject of the right to rule* (tōchiken no shutai) *lies in the Emperor—this is our* kokutai's *fundamental principle and the absolute unshakable conviction of the Empire's subjects. The spirit and content of the Constitution's Introduction and articles make it clear. But to take such theory from another country without any reason and apply it to our* kokutai, *after which the subject of the right to rule lies not in the Emperor but in the state and that the Emperor is an organ of the state, this so-called Emperor organ theory goes in an extreme way against our sacred* kokutai *and violates its fundamental principle and therefore must be rooted out harshly* (gen ni sanjo sezaru bekarazu). *Because politics, religion and all other areas [in Japan] are based on our fundamental*

kokutai *principle, which is unique among all nations, it becomes therefore
necessary to clarify its substance.*[159]

To "clarify the *kokutai* substance" and remove the Minobe state view from the
higher schools' curricula, the Ministry of Education set up an 'Educational
Reform Committee' (*kyōgaku sasshin hyōgikai*) in November 1935, to which
Hiraizumi was added as a participant.[160] Hiraizumi mostly didn't comment on
politics and current events in his writings, and only decades after the war he
expressed his strong disdain for Minobe, whom he singled out as being
responsible for the perceived ills that had gripped Japan during the liberal
phase of *Taishō Democracy*.[161]

2. 3. 'The February 26 Incident'

On the cold and snowy morning of 26 February 1936, when Hiraizumi arrived for his periodical lecture at the Naval War College, he heard about the ongoing *coup d'état* attempt taking place by a group of junior rank army officers and their units, altogether 1500 men, who in the early morning occupied the Parliament, the Army Ministry and Police Headquarters and murdered several members of the elite, including Finance Minister Takahashi Korekiyo (1854-1936) and former Prime Minister and current Lord Keeper of the Privy Seal Saitō Makoto (1858-1936).[162] In their 'Uprising Manifesto' (*Kekki shuisho*), the twenty-two officers demanded political reforms in accordance with the *kokutai*:

> *Now, as we are faced with great emergencies both foreign and domestic, if we do*
>
> *not execute the disloyal and unrighteous who threaten the kokutai, if we do not cut*
>
> *away the villains who obstruct the Emperor's authority, who block the Restoration,*
>
> *the Imperial plan for our nation will come to nothing ... To cut away the evil*
>
> *ministers and military factions near the Emperor and destroy their heart: that is*
>
> *our duty and we will complete it.*[163]

Prince Chichibu, who currently served in the »Thirty First Infantry Division« in Hirosaki (Aomori Prefecture), immediately asked his division commander for permission to return to Tōkyō. As he departed with his own special train, the commander informed Prince Takamatsu by telephone who then called Hiraizumi on the morning of the 27th—when martial law was declared in Tōkyō—and asked him to meet Chichibu halfway, on his way to the capital. At Minakami station (Gunma Prefecture), Hiraizumi was allowed to board

Chichibu's train where they spoke until they arrived together in Tōkyō in the evening and the Prince was ushered to the Palace through a secure gate.[164]

There was much speculation about their conversation on the train and Hiraizumi's possible connection to the revolt. Hiraizumi had idealized the Imperial system in his weekly private lecture for Chichibu from March 1932 to July 1933, when he, as he later noted, laid out to him "the great directive of the Imperial generations' political rule ... by putting emphasis on clarifying its sublime spirit." Chichibu though kept entertaining 'revolutionary ideas' and 'militaristic views' that didn't please the throne and apparently urged his brother Hirohito after the *May 1932 Revolt* to initiate a *Shōwa Restoration*.[165] The reason why he headed back to Tōkyō on 26 February 1936 was said to be his sympathy with the rebels' cause, some of whom he knew personally. Hiraizumi kept his silence about their talk on the train. After the war he said that he had urged him to follow Hirohito's command and refrain from any independent action.[166] In his meeting with Hirohito on the evening of the 27th, Chichibu indeed seemed to have distanced himself from the plotters, as Hirohito mentioned on the following day to one palace official:

Prince Takamatsu's behavior was the best; Prince Chichibu's attitude has widely improved since the May Fifteen [1932] Incident.[167]

The crisis situation went on for two more days. On the 28th, an Imperial order to end the 'rebellion' (*hanran*) was ignored by the rebels. On that evening, Hiraizumi called two trusted officers from the *Seiseijuku* to his house. One of them, Lieutenant Iwata Masataka (1912-2004), later claimed that Hiraizumi had resolved to convince the rebel leaders to surrender by sacrificing his own life if necessary and asked Iwata to assist him on his mission. Anticipating his certain death on the next day, Iwata spent the night writing his last will.[168] Their assignment however wasn't necessary because the Army suppressed the rebellion on the 29th and arrested the ringleaders and several civilians involved, including Kita who was seen as the influencer behind the scenes. Iwata too had initially been an adherent of Kita's *Outline Plan for the Reorganization of Japan*, but eventually followed Hiraizumi and joined the *Seiseijuku* in 1935.[169]

During these days of emergency in late February 1936, Hiraizumi suggested to Prince Takamatsu that a cabinet led by Prince Konoe would have the authority to restore order and govern closely to the ideal of *Personal Imperial Rule*, meaning a non-parliamentary regime connected to the Throne. Hiraizumi formulated his proposals for political restructuring in a text he called the »Peafowl Memorandum« (*Kujakuki*) and gave it Konoe, who now was seen as the most likely next prime minister.[170] But Konoe made himself unavailable and the Imperial order went to the career diplomat Hirota Kōki (1878-1848) who formed his cabinet on March 9th 1936.

As Hirota was selecting his cabinet members, a rumor circulated in the Army that Hiraizumi would be the next Minister for Education.[171] But Hiraizumi soon noticed a growing dislike for him, as he was seen somehow partly responsible for the *February 26 Incident*. He fell out of favor with the Court group when Yuasa became new Lord Keeper of the Privy Seal for the assassinated Saitō. Yuasa had an open aversion for Hiraizumi, much to Konoe's regret who still kept him in high regard and consulted him several times in political matters. The Imperial Navy canceled all of Hiraizumi's teaching engagements, except for the Engineering College in Maizuru, where Matsudaira Yoshitami's son Nagayoshi graduated the next year.[172]

The *February 26 Incident* marked the end for reform calls through a *Shōwa Restoration*. The Army's technocratic 'Control Faction' (*tōseiha*) imposed itself on the Hirota cabinet and used the *February 26 Incident* to deprive it's rivaling 'Imperial Way Faction' of their influence. The rebellion leaders were tried in a secret Special Court Martial (*tokusetsu gunpō kaigi*) that went on for months. The Military Police (*kenpeitai*) investigated Hiraizumi's *Seiseijuku*, as some members—mostly junior or middle rank Army officers—were suspected to have ties with the rebels and the dividing line between the radical '*Kokutai* Fundamentalist Faction' (*kokutai genriha*), their protecting senior officers in the *Imperial Way Faction* and the *Seiseijuku* group was often not clear.[173]

After Hiraizumi clarified his own position in a presentation (titled "The Japanese Spirit's Divine Essence") at the Military Police Headquarters on 10 June 1936, the Army sent several officers, who had been previously involved in the *May 15 Incident*, to the *Seiseijuku* for 'reeducation'. The Military Police however kept scrutinizing the *Seiseijuku* as Hiraizumi complained to Prince Takamatsu in May 1937.[174]

61

Hiraizumi Kiyoshi

Tōjō Hideki

Kikuchi Takeo

Konoe Fumimaro

3. The Road into War, 1937-1941

In July 1936—at the 600-years-anniversary of the *Battle of Minato River*—Hiraizumi formed a study group, 'The *Kenmu*-Principle Society' (*Kenmugikai*), that pledged to uphold the *Japanese loyalist spirit* as the highest ethical norm by rejecting Western positivistic historical thinking. The society started the monthly journal *Kenmu*, edited by Hiraizumi's assistants Matsumoto Ayao (1913-1978) and Nagoya Tokimasa (1915-2005). Over the summer of 1936, the group built a Shintō Shrine in Kamiōsaki (Tōkyō/Shinagawa) dedicated to Godaigo's followers, named the *Kenmu* Shrine (*Kenmu jinja*).[175] Hiraizumi then made his first short vacation since his return to Japan in 1931, after which he had burdened himself with an intense work schedule. In the autumn of 1936, he published the book *Banbutsu ruten* (»All Things Flow«) to prove the existence of an unalterable principle—'the everlasting true'—in the transient world of constant flux as stated by Heraclitus. He began:

Studying history is a sad task because of the validity of the iron principle that all things change. ... The Greek philosopher [Heraclitus] called it 'panta rhei', the [ancient] wise thinkers in India called it 'aniccā vata sankhārā' [jp. shogyō mujō: 'nothing stays the same'].... Isn't that evident for all of history? When everything constantly changes, there can't be anything or any principle to rest on as a result. Doesn't therefore human life become empty and void in this constant flow? No! No! Human life means that there is an unalterable law preserved in the flow and an everlasting true in the transient.[176]

To claim an objective eternal truth in history, he invoked an Archimedean 'fixed point' (*Punctum Archimedes*), as laid out to him in Berlin by professor Meinecke ("what we adhere to"). Hiraizumi declared:

> *When we see that the things are incessantly in flux as Heraclitus did, then we have no choice but to desperately rely on Archimedes to give us a fixed position as a standing ground.*[177]

This *eternal static position* — so Hiraizumi — was the "everlasting moral principle of loyalty and filialty (*chūkō*), … the law that penetrates into the depth of human life." He simply used the Neo-Confucian dual value structure for his historical-philosophical synthesis, from which he elevated *loyalty* to be the primary principle by connecting it to the presence of an 'eternal law' that made *loyalty* towards the Emperor for all subjects into a commandment of total devotion that ultimately meant "to calmly await death at any time":[178]

> *To submit to death. This is lightly said but hard to carry out. … It must be practiced with a courageous spirit until it becomes normal in everyday life. Only then … one doesn't fear danger anymore and can resolutely follow the right path. … It teaches that those who don't comply with the [superficial] crowd, but instead with the way of loyalty and filialty and therefore give their lives with ease, do not cling to wealth or status and moreover are able to live for a moment in the highest form of emotions.*

> *Loyalty and filialty are the utmost of the way and the beginning of all learning. To walk this way all through to its end teaches the eternal moral commandments. With its study the first step into the laborious practice begins. Then the shallow, pleasant and volatile life will be recognized as transitory and one is no longer beguiled by its passing appearance because of its irrelevancy. It's of course difficult to accept the eternal everlasting morality in the endless flow of things and it's even harder to walk the way of loyalty and filialty. Those who follow the way … must endure many hardships.*[179]

The "loyal death (*chūshi*) in the *Kusunoki* spirit" conveyed for Hiraizumi the "absolute immutable highest principle ... how one should throw his life away", as it would lead to 'eternal life' (*eien no seimei*) in the transient world: "Being imbued with the way's true principle means to attain eternal life."[180] He didn't explain this further, but considering his Shintō family background, *eternal life* would mean the soul's continuing existence as a Shintō spirit (*kami*). Hiraizumi focused on Maki Izumi (Maki Yasuomi, 1813-1864), a *Mito* School acolyte who wrote the treatise *Nanshiron* (»About Kusunoki«), in which he placed Kusunoki's highest virtue on the fact that he not only had sacrificed himself for the Emperor but also demanded the same from his descendants, that's why the Kusunoki clan ceased to exist in the fourteenth century. This, according to Maki, "is the way for all generations to follow." Maki summed up the priority of loyalty towards the Emperor before any other obligation in the phrase: "It suffices when the Imperial line continues."[181]

Yasui Eiji (1890-1982), a top official who became governor of Ōsaka in 1935, implemented Hiraizumi's ideology into the Kansai area's school curriculum. To train teachers and policemen in the *Kusunoki spirit* he built a lecture facility near the remnants of Kusunoki's fortress Chihaya on Mount Kongō. Constructed in early 1333, Chihaya was Kusunoki's operational base in Kawachi Province to fight the Hōjō forces while Godaigo was away in exile. A large army besieged the fortifications—that consisted of simple wood and mud structures—without success because of Kusunoki's innovative defense tactics. From there he turned his guerrilla war with only a small number of warriors into the offensive that brought down the Kamakura Shogunate.[182]

On Hiraizumi's advice, Yasui named the Chihaya academy »The House of the Way's Existence« (*Sondōkan*) in reference to Maki's *Nanshiron*. They modeled it after the famous *Mito* academy—»The House to Expand the Way« (*Kōdōkan*) that *Mito* Lord Tokugawa Nariaki (1800-1860) had created in 1841 to teach traditional values as well as martial arts. Inspired by the *Kōdōkan* entrance stone tablet (*Kōdōkanki*), whose inscription was written by Nariaki after a draft by the scholar Fujita Tōko, Yasui ordered a similar tablet from a *Mito* quarry using the same type of granite. Hiraizumi formulated the inscription:

Here we remember General Kusunoki, who in purest loyalty and deepest sincerity … right on this very place, raised the [Imperial] banner and repulsed … a strong enemy … to reestablish more than half a year later the Imperial government according to ancient rule. Not only this, but who also during the country's later emergency suffered with his whole clan, the loyal death and demonstrated to all subjects in the Imperial Land the right way how to preserve the lifeline of the state for eternity. From this aspect, none of the three thousand castles in our country comes close to the fortress Chihaya. … [The Sondōkan] intends to train heroic talents and allows them to dive deeply into Kusunoki's magnificent spirit, so that they strengthen in this time of ideological chaos the Imperial subject's path and follow in this age of egoism and seduction the loyal spirit of the wise men that had come before us (sentetsu), *… with the purpose to protect the state forever.*[183]

Konoe invited Hiraizumi to his Karuizawa residence in October 1936. During their conversation, Konoe got a telephone call about the ongoing negotiations for the 'Anti-Comintern Pact' (*bōkyō kyōtei*) with Nazi Germany that would be signed in Berlin on 25 November 1936. Konoe described the pact to Hiraizumi as a "huge diplomatic success for Japan … since it's intolerable that Great Britain and America control the whole world." He asked Hiraizumi to write the speech which he read as President of the House of Peers on January 17th 1937 at the opening session of the newly constructed National Diet Building in Tōkyō.[184]

Soon after the start of the new session, Army Minister Terauchi Hisaichi (1879-1946) resigned on January 23rd 1937 after a heated clash — the so-called '*harakiri* debate' (*harakiri mondō*) — with the parliamentarian Hamada Kunimatsu (1868-1939), who called out the Army's increasing interference into politics. With his resignation Terauchi caused the downfall of the Hirota cabinet that dissolved on the same day. Expecting Konoe to head the next government, Hiraizumi sent him a 'Ten Point Proposal' for a new political approach.[185]

Instead, General Ugaki Kazushige (1868-1956) was chosen to form a cabinet. The Army command however rejected Ugaki because of his decisions as Army Minister during the *March 1931 Incident* when he had decided to arrest the involved officers, so the generals blocked his cabinet building by refusing to appoint a candidate for the Army Ministry who—after just recently revised rules—had to be an active serving general. Since under the Meiji Constitution the cabinet couldn't function without a minister for each military branch, Ugaki wasn't able to set up his cabinet. This kind of obstruction was unprecedented since the Army on the other hand, was not supposed to interfere with the Emperor's decisions for government. Konoe called Hiraizumi by telephone with the request to draft a letter to acting Army Minister Terauchi to remind the Army of its role under the Constitution. With only a minor amendment, Konoe sent Hiraizumi's letter to Terauchi. It went:

As I read in the news how the Army after several internal meetings voiced its refusal [to accept] the Imperial mandate towards General Ugaki [to form a new government] ... I have to make a basic comment regarding politics [in our country]; rejecting a person, who is chosen by Imperial order, is extraordinary in view of the highest principle. ... Because the state functions according to the system of principle and order (taigi meibun); *and if this is disturbed in even a small way, all order may collapse and chaos might break loose in the future.*[186]

But the Army kept stalling until Ugaki finally gave up and General Hayashi Senjūrō (1876-1943) formed a new cabinet that lasted only four months. When Konoe eventually took over the government on June 4th 1937, Hiraizumi wrote a poem of celebration:

> *The thick fog clears up*
> *And the morning may arise*
> *When the Road of the Imperial Land begins to appear.*[187]

On Hiraizumi's recommendation, Konoe appointed Yasui as Minister for Education, but Yasui soon faced opposition when he tried to install his own faction in the ministerial bureaucracy. On July 5th 1937, the secret military trials for the *February 26 Insurrection* announced their verdicts—mostly death sentences. Yasui and Hiraizumi urged Konoe to pardon some of the officers. This move hardened the bureaucrats' objection towards Yasui until Konoe replaced him in October with Kido.[188]

3. 1. Professorships for the
History of Japanese Thought

The 'Emperor Organ Theory Controversy' (*tennō kikansetsu jiken*) in 1935 led to an adjustment of higher education in line with the *kokutai* state dogma that dominated the basic school curriculum since the Meiji-period but couldn't get a hold in the academic discourse. The *Educational Reform Committee* submitted its report in the fall of 1936. It suggested to turn schools into '*kokutai* based training centers' and universities should set up special 'professorial chairs for *kokutai* research' (*kokutaigaku kōza*) to ground the humanities in the state ideology.[189] Since the *kokutai* concept remained unspecified overall, a group of academics—Hiraizumi was not involved—was called to produce an official text which became the book *Kokutai no hongi* (»Fundamentals of Our National Polity«) that was distributed to all schools and universities in April 1937.[190]

In February 1937, Colonel Tsuji Masanobu (1902-1968) came to Hiraizumi with the request to help creating a state university in the puppet state Manchukuo, where future Manchurian and Chinese officials would be trained in the Japanese Pan-Asian worldview. The university was the idea of Colonel Ishiwara Kanji (1889-1949), the mastermind of the *Manchurian Incident*, who currently served in the General Staff Headquarters (*sanbō honbu*). Ishiwara assigned his confidant Lt. General Itagaki Seishirō, the *Guandong*-Army's Chief of Staff, to begin with the preparations. Itagaki had just read Hiraizumi's book *Chū to gi* and decided to offer him the position as the university's rector. Hiraizumi declined but agreed to select the candidates for the teaching positions.[191]

When Itagaki was transferred to Hiroshima in March 1937 to command the »Fifth Infantry Division« (*daigo shidan*) he called Hiraizumi for a lecture (topic: "The Moral Principle of the Imperial Land", *kōkoku no dōgi*) and to discuss the academy's structure which was named *Manshū kenkoku daigaku* (»Manchu State Building University«). Hiraizumi wanted a new type of ideologically confined academy, where—"in accordance with the *kokutai*"—all liberal and leftist tendencies, as prevalent in the Japanese universities, would be suppressed from the start. He suggested to build and closely supervise dormitories and complementary drill schools (*juku*) on the campus "for *kokutai* based character development" by permitting the students no privacy to prevent them from straying from the approved line of thinking.[192]

Hiraizumi asked the Shintō scholar Kakei Katsuhiko (1872-1961), the economist Sakuta Shōichi (1878-1973) and the philosophy professor Nishi Shin'ichirō (1873-1943) to organize the faculty departments. It briefly came to a disagreement with the *Guandong*-Army's plan to install the moderate Lt. General Ushijima Sadao (1876-1960) as rector, to whom Hiraizumi strongly objected. When he threatened to leave the project, General Honjō Shigeru (1876-1945) and Lt. General Tōjō Hideki visited him and persuaded him to attend the inaugural conference in Xinjing that was led by Tōjō in July 1937. After Hiraizumi's arrival in Manchukuo, Tsuji informed him about the 'Incident at the Marco Polo Bridge' (*Rokōkyō jiken*) that had just occurred a few days ago on July 7th near Beiping (Beijing) and over the next weeks would lead to full scale war with China. Tsuji took Hiraizumi on a trip through Manchukuo before Emperor Pu Yi read the *Manchu State Building University* opening decree on August 5th.[193]

In the autumn of 1937, the *Educational Reform Committee* debated the format of the required 'professorial chairs for *kokutai* research.' Hiraizumi insisted in these meetings to merge them with the 'Shintō chairs' (*Shintō kōza*) that had been formed in 1934. To circumvent the problem that the *kokutai* thought tradition offered insufficient academic substance, the committee decided to broaden their range under the new title 'chairs for the history of Japanese thought' (*Nihon shisōshi kōza*) while the Shintō chairs would be simultaneously enlarged as well. *Professorships for the History of Japanese Thought* were installed in all Imperial universities in the spring of 1938 and the committee left it to Hiraizumi—who wasn't happy about it—to organize and lead the new chair at Tōkyō Imperial University in addition to his primary field of *Japanese Medieval History*.[194]

Hiraizumi picked the lecturers and assistants from his *Seiseijuku* and *Shukōkai* members. Their research in *Japanese Thought History* consisted mainly of editing 'loyalist writings' from the Edo period. As his first project over the summer of 1938, Hiraizumi assigned the student Terada Takeshi (1912-1990) to collect the texts of the *Mito* follower Ōhashi Totsuan (1816-1862), about whom Terauchi had written his graduation thesis. Ōhashi had postulated a defense policy against the Europeans similar to Yoshida Shōin and was eventually arrested for his involvement in the assassination attempt on the Shogunate Elder Andō Nobumasa (1819-1871) by six *Mito* samurai at the Sakashita Gate at Edo Castle in February of 1862, after which he died in prison. Hiraizumi published the First volume of the »Collected Works of Master Ōhashi Totsuan« (*Ōhashi Totsuan sensei zenshū*) and sent Terada at the end of 1938 to the *Manchu State Building University* as an assistance professor.[195]

Hiraizumi started the compilation of a »Japan Studies Anthology« (*Nihongaku sōsho*) that in time stretched to thirteen volumes and comprised mostly *Kimon-*, *kokugaku-* and *Mito*-texts. In the fall of 1938, he supervised the edition of three volumes: »*Nihongaku sōsho 4*« on the 'warrior's creed' (*bukyō*) with two texts by Yamaga Sokō (*Bukyō honron* and *Bukyō shōgaku*) and one by Yoshida Shōin (*Bukyō zensho kōroku*); »*Nihongaku sōsho 8*« with three central *Mito* treatises by Fujita Tōko (*Kōdōkan kijutsugi*), Fujita Yūkoku (*Seimeiron*) and Aizawa Yasushi (*Kyūmon ihan*); and »*Nihongaku sōsho 2*« with two discourses on Emperor loyalism by Kuriyama Senpō (*Hōken taiki*) and his disciple Tani Jinzan (*Hōken taiki uchigi*).[196]

With professor Tsuji Zennosuke (1877-1955) retiring in March 1938, Hiraizumi became the head of the Department for Japanese History. He now occupied the 'First Professorial Chair' (*kokushi dai'ichi kōza*) while the vacant 'Second Chair' went to Nakamura Kōya (1885-1970), a nationalistic scholar who specialized in the same field as he: In 1934 Nakamura published a book titled »A Review of the *Kenmu* Restoration« (*Kenmu no chūkō no kaiko*), followed in 1935 by a Kusunoki biography and a propagandistic discourse about »National Defense and the Japanese Spirit« (*Kokubō to Nihon seishin*).[197] Nakamura hated Hiraizumi,—likely because he had been bypassed by the 10-years younger

Hiraizumi for position as a full professor in 1935—but they worked together in 1938 to organize the 600-years-commemoration events for Nitta Yoshisada and Kitabatake Akiie (1318-1338).[198] Maruyama Masao (1914-1996)—one of the leading authorities in political science at Tōkyō University after the war—saw Hiraizumi crying during his lecture about Nitta:

> *This was some kind of a lecture! When talking about Nitta Yoshisada's loyalty towards Emperor Godaigo, he burst out into tears! (Laughed) I was there just for listening but according to his students, Hiraizumi led them fail in tests when they wrote the name of Ashikaga Takauji with the [correct] character* taka [meaning: 'high respect']. *They had to use [another]* taka *because he was a traitor. ... And they had to add the [honorific noble title]* kyō *to Kitabatake Chikafusa's name. Without it they were in trouble. It was this type of "History of Japanese Thought."* (Laughed)[199]

Kikuchi Takeo, who had risen to prominence in patriotic circles after his role in defaming professor Minobe in 1935, founded a 'Society to extol the Kikuchi loyalism' (*Kikuchishi kinnō kenshōkai*) and asked Hiraizumi to write his family history. He was a descendant of the medieval Kikuchi clan from Higo Province (Kyūshū) that had fought against the Mongol invasions under Kikuchi Takefusa (1245-1285) and then sided with Godaigo under Kikuchi Taketoki (1292-1333) and Kikuchi Takemitsu (1319-1373). The Kikuchi were eventually defeated by the Ōuchi, who were aligned with the Ashikaga, and driven into exile in the remote area Mera (Miyazaki Prefecture). Kikuchi Takeo was the grandson of Mera Noritada (1831-1908), who supported the loyalists around Maki Izumi and sent a confidant to Kyōto in 1863 to form an Imperial militia which brought him into trouble with the Tokugawa regime. The Meiji government granted Noritada for his service the surname Kikuchi along with the nobility rank of Baron (*danshaku*). Hiraizumi accepted Kikuchi's request and travelled to Kyūshū in the summer of 1938.[200]

3. 2. Expanding on the Philosophy of Death

The Konoe government hoped to end the war in China with the capture of the capital of Nanjing in December 1937—where the Japanese military committed large-scale atrocities—but the Chinese Nationalists under Chiang Kaishek (1887-1975) pledged to continue to fight and retreated westwards. In the ensuing Battle of Tai'erzhuang in March/April 1938, the Imperial Army suffered its first defeat and the conflict began to consume more and more men and resources.[201] Hiraizumi now became a spokesman for the ideal of the heroic death on the battlefield. In a long lecture over several days in the »Army's Military Police School« (*rikugun kenpei gakkō*) in February/March 1938 he connected his familiar theme of the *loyalist spirit* with the destiny of the Empire of Japan. Kusunoki's self-sacrifice, he claimed, sparked the *Kimon* and *Mito* tradition into being, with its lineage from Yamazaki Ansai and Yamaga Sokō to Hashimoto Keigaku and Yoshida Shōin all motivated by his heroism, which has to be the everyday standard for every Japanese "to be ready to defend the *kokutai* with one's life at any given time":

> *The* kokutai *[Imperial System] could only persist throughout history because it was preserved precisely by the deeds of many loyalists who threw away their lives in countless struggles. … When somebody is moved by the* kokutai *and wants to protect it with his own life, he must absolutely inhale the loyal spirit from the* Kenmu *era. And he must accept the Kimon teaching as science! He must be filled with it! It's an extraordinary teaching! … If one doesn't internalize it deeply … he can't serve the [nation].*[202]

The self-sacrifice in the *Kimon* spirit is the essence of all 'true science':

True service is in the end nothing else than the self-sacrifice for the [eternal] Way. It means to give body and life for the Way. So, the problem lies in clarifying what the Way is? This is the essence of science. Clarifying the Way equals science. Over time, the meaning of science has changed to attain knowledge or to accumulate expertise with the aim to achieve status [in society] but the essential mission of science is to study the Way. To learn from the ancients is called … practice (keiko). *Kitabatake explained this several times in the* Jinnō shōtōki. *… The fact that our intellectual world has fallen so deeply into disarray lies within the fact that the science [in our country] since the Meiji era has abandoned this old practice. To practice means to train the self in the time-honored traditions. When asked as a Japanese, what character our country has, why it originated, what history it has, by whom our miraculous history and our great* kokutai *has unfolded and is protected, one can never understand the Way if he doesn't inhale … this spirit.*[203]

The Meiji Restoration came about because of the *Kusunoki spirit*:

[The spirit of the Meiji Restoration] … means nothing else than the return of Kusunoki's spirit. The most honored man by the loyalists I have mentioned—in whose spirit they acted—was Kusunoki. Finding back to him and exercising his spirit was exactly what the loyalists did during the Meiji Renewal. … When Kusunoki finally cut his stomach in the Battle of Minato River he swore to return seven times to destroy the traitors. One of his reincarnations was Hashimoto, another one was Yoshida, and all the other loyalists at the end of the Shogunate era were born precisely to continue his spirit.[204]

He quoted Yoshida, who—just before his execution in 1859—grounded the *Japanese morality* in a cult of death:

[Yoshida said:] "When all Japanese have the spirit of sacrificing their lives for their country and when all the subjects give their lives for His Majesty, when this morality is set up, there's no reason to fear the foreign nations. Today the most important task is to build this Japanese morality! You die as a human being for

your parents and you die as a subject for the ruler! When this morality stands, nobody must fear the other countries. Don't we all want to use all of our strength to establish this morality?" Master Yoshida spoke these lines in prison. What splendid words![205]

In a talk before police officials, Hiraizumi divided the history of Japan in periods of 'light' and 'darkness:' The *light* shone in the Heian period, when the Emperor ruled according to the ancient sacred decree. The *darkness* came with the feudal system, "when people didn't comprehend the *kokutai*." The *light* reappeared in Godaigo's short-lived *Kenmu* phase, when the loyalists fought hopeless battles for the *high principle* and manifested the *pure Japanese spirit* as a guiding light for later generations. This spirit turned into 'bright light' in the Meiji Restoration, but it also has to be nurtured constantly and continuously by every Japanese to not let the nation fall back into dark times.[206]

When Konoe told to him in April 1938 his intention to resign as Prime Minister, Hiraizumi tried to dissuade him and even visited Prince Chichibu to encourage him to stay in office.[207] Konoe eventually reshuffled his cabinet and continued to govern for eight more months. On November 3rd, he proclaimed a 'New Order in East Asia' (*Tōa shinchitsujo*) to ideologically underline and justify Japan's war of aggression.

Hiraizumi duly inserted expansionary elements into his historical narration. He pointed to Hashimoto's 'pioneering plan' at the end of the Tokugawa period that envisioned the conquest of Korea and Manchuria, followed by setting up Japanese colonies in India and America, while 'neutralizing' Great Britain and Russia through temporary alliances to eventually fight the Western powers one by one. This plan, Hiraizuimi stated, became reality with the occupation of Manchuria in 1931, now Japan has to pursue its destiny by advancing further. He cited Maki who—inspired by the *Mito* School's anti-foreign *sonnō-jōi* view—had set the goal of 'Imperial Rule over the Whole World' (*udai ittei*). Hiraizumi concluded: "That's the supreme ideal in the Imperial Land. We die to turn it into reality. ... We all have the same duty to give our lives for it".[208]

He fully embraced the official slogan; 'Eight Corners under One Roof' (*hakkō ichiu*) — meaning also the Empire's worldwide expansion — that rapidly became in vogue in 1938. Initially the term was used by Tanaka Chigaku (1861-1939), a religious leader of the 'Nichirenism Sect' (*Nichiren shugi*), who picked it from the *Nihon shoki* to propagate a moral and benevolent enlargement of the Imperial state with the objective of world unification based on his reading of the teachings of the medieval Buddhist monk Nichiren (1222-1282).[209] Until the 1930s the phrase was still confined to Tanaka's movement, that's why Hiraizumi had touched on it only briefly in his commentary to a *Nihon shoki* edition in 1934.[210] It finally gained wide attention when the government named it as an objective of the 'National Spiritual Mobilization Movement' (*kokumin seishin sōdōin undō*) — that was jointly organized by the Ministry of Home Affairs and Ministry of Education in October 1937 and headed by Admiral Arima — to provide an ideological base for the war on the continent.

At a gathering of the *Imperial Military Reservist Association* on January 25th 1939, Hiraizumi explained the *hakkō ichiu* concept as the 'Principle for the Way' (*dōgi*) that had guided Emperor Jinmu during his 'creation of the [ancient Japanese] state' (*chōkoku*) to become the 'eternal Japanese morality', but which "also comprises a mandate to save China through the morally supreme *bushidō* principle" — meaning the Japanese military — to merge all nations into Japan's hierarchical 'family system' (*kazoku shugi*), lauded by Hiraizumi as a "just ruling system ... that categorically excludes all international liberalism."[211] In February/March 1939 he held seven seminars in the Foreign Ministry about the "wide and just principle of *hakkō ichiu*" that commands Japan to expand into the world.[212]

On 27th December 1938, Hiraizumi received the official request from the Konoe government to join the research project to determine the 'sacred historical sites' related to Emperor Jinmu in preparation for the upcoming nationwide celebrations of the '2600th Anniversary of the Japanese Empire' (*kigen nisen roppyakunen kinen*) in 1940.[213] The committee held its first large meeting sessions on 10-11 February 1939 and announced an initial set of locations — Kashihara Shrine and Mt. Kama in Wakayama Prefecture — as being associated to Jinmu's mythical reign. Kenneth Ruoff wrote:

The committee's task was to investigate whether or not the precise location of thirty-six place names related to Emperor Jinmu mentioned in the Kojiki *or* Nihon shoki *could be determined with a degree of surety that would justify the construction of stone monuments designating the sites as sacred national landmarks. The committee was provided with substantial authority to rule on which sites merited official recognition.*[214]

Meanwhile in January 1939, a conflict escalated in the Economic Faculty of Tōkyō Imperial University between the liberal group of professor Kawai Eijirō (1891-1944) and the advocates of a state-controlled economic system akin to the totalitarian dictatorships in Europe around faculty leader Hijikata Seibi (1890-1975). When Kawai and four of his supporters submitted their resignations, the new rector Vice Admiral Hiraga Yuzuru (1878-1943) ordered Hijikata also to retire which prompted nine academics of his faction to resign as well. This 'Hiraga Purge' (*Hiraga shukugaku*) sparked right-wing groups into action and twelve students of Hiraizumi's *Shukōkai* signed a petition with their blood to keep the Hijikata group in their positions. The *Shukōkai* had grown from 27 members in 1932 to 86 in 1939 and organized speeches on the campus. In January 1939 they invited the Indian political activist Rash Behari Bose, in June 1939 the commander responsible for the Nanjing Massacre, General Matsui Iwane (1878-1948).[215]

On April 4th, a commemoration event for the '700th Anniversary of Emperor Gotoba's Death' was held in the Yoyogi Youth Hall. Gotoba had challenged the Kamakura Shogunate in the *Jōkyū* War in 1221 and subsequently died in exile in 1239. Hiraizumi delivered a speech in the presence of Prince Chichibu together with Kido, who currently served as Minister of the Interior in the Hiranuma cabinet that was formed in January when Konoe left office.[216] Hiraizumi then travelled with Kikuchi to his country estate in Miyazaki to research the Kikuchi family history.[217] During the summer and autumn, he joined the field investigation as part of the *Commission of Inquiry into Historical Sites Related to Emperor Jinmu* and evaluated together with his academic colleagues fourteen locations in the Kansai region (Ōsaka/Nara).[218] Ruoff noted:

Most professors who were members of the committee participated in various field visits in 1939 and 1940. Rather than completing research on all the candidate locations and then rendering a decision, the committee issued its conclusions on various locations with a series of announcements over eighteen months. Whether intended or not, this method added considerable drama to the work of the committee because each announcement, on which hung the hopes of various localities, was a major media event.[219]

Back in Tōkyō, Hiraizumi attended the '600th Anniversary of Emperor Godaigo's Death' on 27 September 1939 in the '*Kudan* Soldiers Hall' (*Kudan gunjin kaikan*), where he spoke together with Kikuchi, Arima, the Shintō researcher Kōno Shōzo (1882-1963) and Education Minister Kawarada Kakichi (1886-1955). Hiraizumi edited a Godaigo book and then departed for a speech tour to several prefectures.[220] In the fall, a group of civil service applicants from the »Datong Academy« (*Datong xueyuan*) in Manchukuo came to him to be instructed in a special seminar course. He taught them how the Empire of Japan embodied the *highest moral principle* through the unbroken Imperial line, which "renders the duty towards the Emperor being without limits." By serving Japan's just mission, he told them, the Manchurian officials will take part in uniting Asia under Japan's guidance.[221] In January 1940, Hiraizumi's new book *Dentō* (»Tradition«) was printed in large numbers. It was a compilation of his speeches and articles that included his previously written texts on 'French Traditionalism'.[222]

3. 3. Konoe's 'New Order', 1940

Hitler's invasion of Poland in September 1939 started World War II in Europe as Great Britain and France declared war on Germany. The Hiranuma cabinet resigned out of irritation over the 'Molotov–Ribbentrop Non-Aggression Pact', after Japan had just fought an undeclared border war with Soviet troops in the summer at Khalkhin Gol in Mongolia—'The Nomonhan Incident' (*Nomonhan jiken*). Hiranuma, who wanted a military alliance with Germany, was replaced by General Abe Nobuyuki (1875-1953), whose administration didn't last very long. In January 1940, with the outcome of the European war still uncertain, Japan's leadership tried a careful approach with Admiral Yonai as Prime Minister who favored a pro-British, pro-American foreign policy. In March, his government scored a propagandistic success when Wang Jingwei (1883-1944), the former second-highest *Guomindang* official, agreed to collaborate with Japan by setting up a regime in Nanjing—'The Reorganized National Government of the Republic of China' (*Nanjing Guomin Zhengfu*). The Japanese sought with this puppet regime the delegitimization of Chiang Kaishek to bring an end to the war in China.

The *Guandong*-Army called Hiraizumi to Manchukuo in March 1940 to deliver six private lectures before Emperor Pu Yi about how the "*kokutai* principle varies morally from China and the West." Hiraizumi detailed to Pu Yi that Japan was the "embodiment of East Asian morality through the intrinsic virtue of its Emperor and faith in the Sun-Goddess Amaterasu," while on the other hand Western individualism and utilitarianism as well as the Chinese principle of *Mandate Change* according to Mengzi were "morally worthless."[223] His tutorials were made in preparation for Pu Yi's second state visit to Japan in June 1940, where he requested from Emperor Hirohito to pray to the Sun-Goddess at Ise Shrine.

> *Emperor Pu Yi came to Japan largely to ask permission from Emperor Hirohito to worship Amaterasu. Emperor Hirohito granted permission for Manchukuo's emperor to worship the progenitor of Japan's imperial line … On the following day, Emperor Pu Yi also worshipped at Kashihara Shrine and at Emperor Jinmu's Mausoleum and other imperial tombs at Mt. Unebi. These rituals were designed to lay the groundwork for the announcement made on 15 July by the government of Manchukuo of its decision that Amaterasu would by worshipped in Manchukuo overall from that time on.*[224]

In the summer of 1940, Hiraizumi held five seminars in the Japanese Foreign Ministry about the *Kenmu Restoration* and "Japan's historical-moral mission in Asia."[225] He felt relieved when Yuasa stepped down as Lord Keeper of the Privy Seal in June to be succeeded by Kido, who praised Hiraizumi as a "like-minded man concerned about the nation" and invited him to his new office on 5th July.[226] The German victory over France shifted the power balance towards the European dictatorships and opened possibilities for Japan to gain hegemony in East Asia. On 24th June—two days after the Franco-German armistice—Konoe announced his intent to create a 'New System' (*shintaisei*), for which he stepped down as chairman of the Privy Council (*sūmitsu'in*).

The Yonai cabinet resigned on July 16th and Konoe was given the order to form his second cabinet. He sent his designated Cabinet Secretary Tomita Kenji to Hiraizumi with the request to write his inauguration speech.[227] As the public debate circled around the anticipated *New System*, which many commentators expected to be a 'national unity party' similar to the totalitarian systems of Nazi-Germany or the Soviet Union, Hiraizumi wanted to emphasize in the speech that political parties in themselves were alien to the nature of the *kokutai*—which was supported by the fact that the *Meiji Constitution* didn't mention any parties nor any politics based on parliamentarism, not even the role of a Prime Minister (*sōri daijin*), but only 'Ministers of the State' (*kokumu daijin*) who were appointed by the Emperor and solely responsible to him. Hiraizumi therefore wrote in the draft that in Japan "there shouldn't be any parties anymore." Konoe read the speech on July 23rd 1940 on radio, but he deleted Hiraizumi's passage about abolishing the existing parties. The speech went:

I recently stepped down as Chairman of the Privy Council because in regards to the serious changes happening in the world I think that the system in our country has to be renewed completely and I want to use all of my energy for this purpose. This is because our nation is [Konoe left out Hiraizumi's line: *"split up into different parties and"*] *divided into various opinions ..., and this kind of friction prevents our strength to be concentrated outwardly as the opportunity for bold decisions gets lost in this aimlessness.*

Two evils exist in the current political parties. Firstly, they're either based on Individualism, Democracy or Socialism with a view towards the world and the human being that is incompatible with the kokutai *and which has to be corrected fast and reformed drastically. Secondly, the whole purpose of a political party is the gain of governmental power, with the result that the legislature doesn't honor the* [Meiji Constitution's] *principle of supporting the Imperial Policy* (taisei yokusan no michi). *I think that these evils must end and everything should return to the true form of Japan* [Hiraizumi: *"follow the* kokutai*"*], *respect the Imperial wish and all the hundred million Japanese have to thoroughly serve the nation.*

[Konoe omitted Hiraizumi's whole next section: *"It's therefore my opinion that the New System shouldn't intend to form a new party by transforming the established parties, but that there shouldn't be any parties anymore. I firmly believe this corresponds with the true* kokutai *principle and I'm glad to already receive approval and support from all sides for this."*]

These problems however persist not only in the political parties but also in the culture, the military ..., the upper and the lower classes. All social hierarchies thus must have only one way of thinking and support [Konoe added: *"the Imperial policy according to"] His Majesty's instructions. It means that everyone in the New System has to obey the Imperial wish and must quickly and properly solve all internal and external challenges relating to the huge historical changes.*[228]

The speech, as intended by Hiraizumi and delivered by Konoe, pointed to the introduction—the 'Promulgation' (*jōyu*)—in the *Meiji Constitution*, where the Emperor expects "to further the prosperity of the State, in concert with Our subjects (*shinmin*) and with their support (*yokusan*)." The Promulgation read:

Having, by virtue of the glories of Our Ancestors, ascended the throne of a lineal succession unbroken for ages eternal; desiring to promote the welfare of, and to give development to the moral and intellectual faculties of Our beloved subjects, the very same that have been favoured with the benevolent care and affectionate vigilance of Our Ancestors; and wishing to further the prosperity of the State, in concert with Our subjects and with their support, We hereby promulgate ... a fundamental law of the State, to exhibit the principles, by which We are guided in Our conduct, and to point out to what Our descendants and Our subjects and their descendants are forever to conform.[229]

The 'Imperial Edict on the Promulgation of the Constitution' (*kenpō happu chokugo*) from February 11th 1889, which most often was read as part of the Constitution's introduction, further stated:

The Imperial Founder of Our House and Our other Imperial Ancestors, by the help and support of the forefathers of Our subjects, laid the foundation of Our Empire upon a basis, which is to last forever. That this brilliant achievement embellishes the annals of Our country, is due to the glorious virtues of Our Sacred Imperial Ancestors, and to the loyalty and bravery of Our subjects, their love of their country and their public spirit. Considering that Our subjects are the descendants of the loyal and good subjects of Our Imperial Ancestors, We doubt not but that Our subjects will be guided by Our views, and will sympathize with all Our endeavours, and that, harmoniously cooperating together, they will share with

Us Our hope of making manifest the glory of Our country, both at home and abroad, and of securing forever the stability of the work bequeathed to Us by Our Imperial Ancestors.[230]

Traditionalists like Uesugi had insisted since the Taishō years that these lines formulated a command from the Imperial Ancestors to all Japanese subjects to unify in collective *support* for the Emperor by ending Parliamentarian Democracy and instead engaging in mass mobilization for a strong standing of the Empire in the world—interpreted in the words "wishing to further the prosperity of the State" (*kokka no shin'un wo fuchi semu koto wo nozomi*) and "they [the subjects] will share with Us Our hope of making manifest the glory of Our country, both at home and abroad."[231] Hiraizumi saw it in the same way. Much later he wrote approvingly how Konoe in 1940 "just followed the true *kokutai* principle, proclaimed the purest traditionalism and bundled all the people into one body to counter the pressing national emergency."[232]

Konoe denied any intention to abolish the existing parties, but the tone he set with his speech about the "evils in the current political parties" and the need to "return to the true form of Japan" through a reformed parliament that accepts its limited constitutional role in primarily obeying the "principle of supporting the Imperial policy" (*taisei yokusan no michi*) gradually over the summer of 1940 increased the pressure on the parties to disband voluntarily, which started with the self-dissolvement of the *Minseitō* (»The Democratic Party«) on August 15th and then followed by all other parties. This led the way for the 'Imperial Rule Assistance Association' (*Taisei yokusankai*) to be proclaimed by Konoe on October 12th, which he explicitly didn't want to conceive as a 'state party' but as a vaguely termed umbrella 'structure' (*kōzō*) that should include every parliamentary faction as well as many other organizations to mobilize the nation to collectively *support* the Imperial policy. To avoid any semblance to a political party Konoe didn't announce a manifesto and called the "program of this movement the practice of the subjects' way (*shindō jissen*)."[233]

With the parliament reduced to a mere acclamation forum for the Imperial government's decisions, Hiraizumi saw the political system back in line with the Meiji Emperor's wishes as laid out in the *Meiji Constitution*. He found his worldview further validated when the Vichy regime under Marshal Philippe Pétain (1856-1951) abandoned the three principles of the French Revolution *liberté-egalité-fraternité* and substituted them with the formula *travail-famille-patrie* ("work-family-homeland") to bring the nation back to traditional values. The death of the last 'Elder Statesman' (*genrō*) Saionji Kinmochi (1849-1940) in November, whose liberal attitude had been formed in his younger years in France, meant for Hiraizumi another end point of the 'upheaval phase' since 1789. [234] On November 30th 1940, a 'Japan-Manchukuo-China Joint Declaration' (*Nichimanka kyōdō sengen*) was signed in Nanjing to bring to bear the "moral based New Order in East Asia" that Konoe had envisioned in his speech two years previously.

Hiraizumi later described 1940 as a "shining year, ... an oasis, the calm before the storm" with its many events celebrating the *2600th Anniversary of the Empire* which peaked in the 'unforgettable' (Hiraizumi) main festival on 10-11 November in Kōkyogaien National Garden at the Imperial Palace in Tōkyō.[235] He then worked on the Kikuchi project and published the book in April 1941: *Kikuchi kinnōshi* (»The History of the Kikuchi Loyalists«). Afterwards, a research committee from Tottori Prefecture asked him to examine the sources on Nawa Nagatoshi, the general who after the *Battle at Minato River* led the remaining Imperial forces against the Ashikaga in Kyōto, where he was killed in the summer of 1336. Hiraizumi also contributed an article for the book *Kōkokugaku taikō* (»The Great Program of Imperial Land Studies«) that professor Kanokogi Kazunobu (1884-1949) from Kyūshū Imperial University (*Kyūshū teikoku daigaku*) edited in the spring of 1941. In his text Hiraizumi summarized his concept of historical science:

That which is called history, ... [usually] means a wide range of depth and shallowness, greatness and triviality. However, in its essential meaning, history is the development of a spirit, meaning the tracing how an ideal is realized. This means that the mere change of the times together with the flux of all things shouldn't be seen as the true nature of history. To understand it as the growth of a spirit and the realization of an ideal two aspects must be considered. Firstly, through pure scientific analysis and pure alignment of source texts it simply can't be discerned how history embodies a spirit, this inevitably happens solely by induction. … Secondly, the spirit-manifestation and ideal-realization aren't based on empty abstract speculations but on careful and exact investigations and considerations.[236]

The Imperial Army's advance into French Indochina in July 1941 triggered the freezing of Japanese assets and an oil embargo by the United States. With tensions increasing between the two nations, Hiraizumi was asked by one scholar—perhaps Kanokogi—to form a group of academics to submit a petition to the Konoe government for a quick declaration of war against the USA, just like the 'Seven Doctors' (*shichi hakushi*) from Tōkyō Imperial University did in 1903 on the eve of the war with Russia. But Hiraizumi didn't want to "undermine the authorities' prudent planning regarding such a serious decision." Shimada Tōsuke, a young Technical Naval Lieutenant, supplied him with news from the Naval Command which he passed on to Konoe.[237] Konoe resigned in mid-October after failing to arrange a meeting with President Roosevelt and was replaced by General Tōjō who steered Japan towards war. On November 5th, the Emperor approved the plan for the attack on Hawaii.

Since the Imperial Navy had cut almost all of its contacts with Hiraizumi after the *February 26 Incident*, Rear Admiral Tokunaga Sakae (1891-1974) from the 'Navy Ministry's Education Bureau' (*kaigunshō kyōikukyoku*) called him back to the higher training schools because he saw an urgent need for an "educational reform of the Navy in the *bushidō* spirit." On November 10th 1941, Hiraizumi held his first lecture before the graduating cadet classes of the Naval Academy in Etajima.[238] A few days later, he was invited to talk before Vice Admiral Nagumo Chūichi (1887-1944) and his staff. Nagumo, who was in command of the 'First Air Fleet' (*dai'ichi kōkū kantai*) that would strike Pearl Harbor three weeks later, didn't say anything about the ongoing war preparations, as Hiraizumi later recalled:

Someone like me absolutely knew nothing about the progress [of the operational plans] and I had no idea about the movements of the military. Though I knew many persons in high positions, they all kept their secrets and when I asked them, they held their distance because they couldn't say anything. For example, Vice Admiral

*Nagumo Chūichi, who led the surprise attack on Pearl Harbor, had been together
with several of his officers as a listener of my lectures for many years. [Now] we
gathered in the quiet officer's room in the Yokosuka Naval District and talked
calmly about the world situation and the prospects for our country. It was very
moving to see Captain Kaku Tomeo to stand up after my lecture and start dancing
without even having drunk any alcohol, with Vice Admiral Nagumo silently
watching the scene while sitting with his back against the blackboard. ... But even
during this gathering Nagumo didn't drop one single word regarding the military's
movements.* [239]

On 27th of November, the Tōjō government received the final proposals by US
Secretary of State Cordell Hull—the 'Hull Note'—which it saw as an
unacceptable ultimatum. The next day, Tomita told Hiraizumi that "it's now
difficult to continue the peace", especially as the USA refused to recognize
the Wang regime in Nanjing.[240] Hiraizumi attended an event for the 'patriotic
philosopher' Asami Keisai (1652-1712) in Ōtsu at lake Biwa. Anticipating that
hostilities against the American forces would be enacted on December 1st, he
mistook a flight exercise over the lake on that day for a sign that the war had
indeed started. The Pearl Harbor attack eventually came a week later on
December 8th (Japanese time zone). For many years, Hiraizumi wondered why
the war hadn't started on *December First* as many informed Japanese in the
higher circles had expected in those days. Finally in the 1960s, Vice Admiral
Shimizu Mitsumi (1888-1971), who commanded the 'Sixth Fleet' (*dairoku
kantai*) against Hawaii, told him that *December Eighth* had been a compromise
with Tōjō who had insisted on the *Fifteenth* as the day for the attack. Because
of the surprise element it had to be a Sunday either way. Shimizu explained
to him:

*The Navy's Commander-in-Chief Yamamoto [Isoroku] demanded December First
to be the day of the decisive attack. But General Tōjō from the Army rejected this
and insisted that it take place on December Fifteenth. [Tōjō's reason was] that
while the Navy could strike instantly with its planes and ships [already in place],
the Army needed trains and transport ships to move their large units of tens of
thousands of men overseas [to South East Asia and the Philippines] and therefore*

couldn't meet the schedule. The Navy wanted December First, the Army wanted December Fifteenth, and since there was no way to resolve it, the compromise was to meet in the middle which meant December Eighth. This secret was only known in the Navy by Admiral Yamamoto, Vice Admiral Nagumo and me, only the three of us.[241]

End of PART ONE

Notes

Introduction

[1] Marius B. JANSEN 2000, *The Making of Modern Japan*, 333.

[2] JANSEN, *The Making of Modern Japan*, 458.

[3] Margaret MEHL, ›German Influence on Historical Scholarship in Meiji Japan‹, in Historiographical Institute at the University of Tokyo 2002, *The Past, Present and Future of History and Historical Sources*, 227-228.

[4] Altered quote after MEHL, ›German Influence on Historical Scholarship in Meiji Japan‹, 227.

[5] Margaret MEHL 2017, *History and the State in Nineteenth-Century Japan: The World, the Nation and the Search for a Modern Past* (2nd Edition), 2-4.

[6] MEHL, *History and the State in Nineteenth-Century Japan*, 108-109.

[7] Kenneth B. PYLE, ›Meiji Conservatism‹, in Bob Tadashi WAKABAYASHI (ed.), *Modern Japanese Thought*, 98-142.

[8] *The Making of Modern Japan*, 395.

[9] Modified quote from ITŌ Hirobumi (trans. by ITŌ Mijoji) 1889, *Commentaries on the Constitution of the Empire of Japan*, 2-7; de BARY, Theodore, GLUCK, Carol, TIEDEMANN, Arthur E. (ed.) 2006, *Sources of Japanese Traditions, Part 2: 1868 to 2000* (Second Edition), 77.

[10] de BARY / GLUCK / TIEDEMANN (ed.), *Sources of Japanese Traditions, Part 2: 1868 to 2000*, 108-109.

[11] See Rieko KAMEI-DYCHE, ›An Engagement with the Scholarship on Mitogaku‹ from the 1930s to the Present‹, 74-146; J. Victor KOSCHMANN 1987, *The Mito Ideology: Discourse, Reform, and Insurrection in Late Tokugawa Japan, 1790-1864*.

[12] See Margaret MEHL, ›Scholarship and Ideology in Conflict: The Kume Affair, 1892‹, in *Monumenta Nipponica*, vol. 48 1993, 337–357; John BROWNLEE 1997, *Japanese Historians and the National Myths, 1600-1945, The Age of the Gods and Emperor Jinmu*, 92-117.

[13] See Lisa YOSHIKAWA 2017, *Making History Matter: Kuroita Katsumi and the Construction of Imperial Japan*.

[14] This book is based on three articles previously published by the author in German: Florian NEUMANN, ›Hiraizumi Kiyoshi und der „Geist" der japanischen Geschichte‹, in *OAG Notizen* 03/2017; Florian NEUMANN, ›Hiraizumi Kiyoshi – Die Kriegsjahre‹, in *OAG Notizen* 04/2018; Florian NEUMANN, ›Hiraizumi Kiyoshi – Die Nachkriegszeit‹, in *OAG Notizen* 09/2019. There are two biographic studies about Hiraizumi, one in Japanese by Wakai Toshiaki and a dissertation in English at the University of Toronto by Ueda Kiyoshi: WAKAI Toshiaki 2006, *Hiraizumi Kiyoshi – Mikuni no tame ni ware tsukusanamu*; UEDA Kiyoshi 2008, *Hiraizumi Kiyoshi (1895-1984): 'Spiritual history' in the Service of the Nation in Twentieth Century Japan*. See also TATAMIYA Eitarō 2000, *Kami no kuni to chōrekishika Hiraizumi Kiyoshi* and the section on Hiraizumi in BROWNLEE, *Japanese Historians and the National Myths, 1600-1945, The Age of the Gods and Emperor Jinmu*, 168-179. Some biographical details are in the introduction by professor Tanaka Takashi for the English translation of Hiraizumi's book *Monogatari Nihonshi* (1979) that was published under the title *The Story of Japan* (vol. 1-3). Hiraizumi himself wrote a long series of personal recollections for one of his journals that he published as the book *Higeki jūsō* (»Passing Through the Tragedy«) in 1980. Together with his many other writings it became the basic source for this study.

[15] See BROWNLEE, *Japanese Historians and the National Myths, 1600-1945*, 71-91.

[16] UEDA Kiyoshi 2008, *Hiraizumi Kiyoshi (1895-1984): 'Spiritual history' in the Service of the Nation in Twentieth Century Japan*, 10.

[17] HAYASHI Kentarō 1960, *Utsuriyuku mono no kage*, cited in TATAMIYA Eitarō 2000, *Kami no kuni to chōrekishika Hiraizumi Kiyoshi*, 57-58.

[18] IROKAWA Daikichi 1968, *Meiji no seishin* (Tōkyō: Chikuma Shobō), cited in TATAMIYA, *Kami no kuni to chōrekishika Hiraizumi Kiyoshi*, 148. Emperor 'Monmu' is falsely quoted. The *Kojiki* was compiled on the order of Emperor Tenmu (ruled 673-686), was probably what Hiraizumi had said.

[19] Tōdai jūhachi shikai (ed.) 1968, *Gakuto shutsujin no kiroku*, 98 pp. Cited in *Kami no kuni to chōrekishika Hiraizumi Kiyoshi*, 149-150.

1. Fukui-Echizen and the 'Kenmu Restoration'

[20] Katsuyamashi (ed.) 2017, *Hakusan Heisenji—yomigaeru shūkyō toshi*, 86-172; HAYATA Yoshihiko, SHIRASAKI Shōichirō, MATSUURA Yoshinori, KIMURA Ryō 2014, *Fukuiken no rekishi (kenshi 18)*, 108-109. There are about 2700 small shrines with the name *Hakusan jinja* in the area.

[21] *Hakusan Heisenji—yomigaeru shūkyō toshi*, 8 pp.

[22] HAYATA, SHIRASAKI, MATSUURA, KIMURA, *Fukuiken no rekishi (kenshi 18)*, 90 pp.

[23] *Fukuiken no rekishi (kenshi 18)*, 109-111. Hiraizumi referred to Dōgen throughout his life.

[24] Helen Craig McCULLOUGH 2008, *The Taiheiki—A Chronicle of Medieval Japan*, xliv.

[25] See Paul VARLEY 1971, *Imperial Restoration in Medieval Japan*; Andrew GOBLE 1996, *Kenmu: Go-Daigos Revolution*. Godaigo took the era name *Kenmu* (chin. *Jianwu*: 'Establishing military might') from the Chinese Emperor Guangwu (5 BC-57 AD) who restored the Han Dynasty after vanquishing the challenger Wang Mang (45 BC-23 AD) who tried to create his own dynasty.

[26] For Kusunoki see Ivan I. MORRIS 2013 (originally 1975), *The Nobility of Failure: Tragic Heroes in the History of Japan*.

[27] MORRIS, *The Nobility of Failure: Tragic Heroes in the History of Japan*, 96.

[28] Eshū's birth name was Kusunoki Magosaburō.

[29] Heisenji jōtōkōtō shōgakkō (ed.) 1935, *Heisenjison kyōdo dokuhon*. (Katsuyama: Takaki insatsujō.) See UEDA, *Hiraizumi Kiyoshi*, 60-61.

[30] Slightly altered translation after Paul H. VARLEY (tr.) 1980, *A Chronicle of Gods and Sovereigns: Jinnō Shōtōki of Kitabatake Chikafusa*, 49.

[31] Andrew Edmund GOBLE, ›Go-Daigō, Takauji, and the Muromachi Shogunate‹, in Karl F. FRIDAY (ed.) 2012, *Japan Emerging: Premodern History to 1850*, 221.

[32] McCULLOUGH, *The Taiheiki—A Chronicle of Medieval Japan*.

³³ Nankō is another name for Kusunoki—*nan* is the Sino-Japanese *on*-reading of the name Kusunoki which means "Camphor Tree."

³⁴ *The Nobility of Failure: Tragic Heroes in the History of Japan*, 102-102.

³⁵ *Fukuiken no rekishi (kenshi 18)*, 150 pp.

³⁶ UEDA, *Hiraizumi Kiyoshi*, 40-41. Gahō eventually backed the validity of the *Northern Court*. For Hayashi Razan see BROWNLEE, *Japanese Historians and the National Myths*, 15-28.

³⁷ *The Nobility of Failure*, 103.

³⁸ For Yamazaki Ansai and the *Kimon* lineage (*ki* is the Japanese *on*-reading of the character *zaki*—meaning "cliff"—in Yamazaki) see Herman OOMS 1985, *Tokugawa Ideology: Early Constructs 1570-1680*, 194-286; NISHI Junzō, ABE Ryūichi, MARUYAMA Masao (ed.) 1980, *Nihon shisō taikei 31: Yamazaki Ansai gakuha*.

³⁹ *Japanese Historians and the National Myths*, 29-41.

⁴⁰ *Ibid.*, 29-30.

⁴¹ *Kami no kuni to chōrekishika Hiraizumi Kiyoshi*, 12-14.

⁴² William E. GRIFFIS 1876, *The Mikado's Empire: Book I, History of Japan, from 660 B.C. to 1872 A.D.*, 190. Matsudaira Munenori (1715-1749), the tenth Lord of Fukui-Echizen, placed a memorial stone for Nitta at the *Shōnenji* temple in Fukui.

⁴³ GRIFFIS, *The Mikado's Empire: Book I*, 191.

⁴⁴ UEDA, *Hiraizumi*, 69.

⁴⁵ ANDŌ Yūichirō 2021, *Echizen Fukui hanshu Matsudaira Shungaku—Meiji ishin wo mezashita Tokugawa ichimon*; UEDA, *Hiraizumi*, 66-71.

⁴⁶ Mainichi shinbun "Yasukuni" shuzaihan (ed.) 2007, *Yasukuni sengo hishi—A-kyūsenpan wo gōshi shita otoko*, 31-53.

⁴⁷ BROWNLEE, *Japanese Historians and the National Myths*, 128. Also see MEHL, *History and the State in Nineteenth-Century Japan* (2nd Edition), 163-171; YOSHIKAWA, *Making History Matter: Kuroita Katsumi and the Construction of Imperial Japan*, 112-121.

⁴⁸ *Japanese Historians and the National Myths*, 128.

⁴⁹ For biographical details see the introduction by professor Tanaka Takashi in the first volume of the English version of Hiraizumi's book *Shōnen Nihonshi* (1970): HIRAIZUMI 1997-2002, *The Story of Japan* (vol. 1-3).

⁵⁰ HIRAIZUMI, *Higeki jūsō*, 425 / 443-447.

⁵¹ Keigakukai (ed.) 1908, *Hashimoto Sanai zenshū*. (Tōkyō: Keigakukai.)

91

[52] UEDA, *Hiraizumi*, 78 pp; WAKAI, *Hiraizumi*, 39-40.

[53] Cited in WAKAI, *Hiraizumi*, 40.

[54] HIRAIZUMI, ›Yoritomo to nengō‹ (›Minamoto Yoritomo and the era names‹), published in the university's historical journal *Shigaku zasshi* 28-10, October 1917. He proposed a new theory on the feudal trade guilds (*za*): HIRAIZUMI, ›Za kanken‹ (›My assessment regarding the *za* guilds‹) in *Shigaku zasshi* 28-12, December 1917; HIRAIZUMI, ›Futatabi za ni tsuite guken wo tsugu‹ (›Again my view about the *za* guilds‹), in *Shigaku zasshi* 29-3, March 1918.

[55] *Higeki jūsō*, 326-327; HIRAIZUMI, ›Ayamararetaru Nikkōbyō‹ (›The misunderstood Nikkō mausoleum‹), in *Shigaku zasshi* 32-2, February 1921; HIRAIZUMI, ›Tokugawa Ieyasu no ikin‹ (›Tokugawa Ieyasu's financial heritage‹), in *Shigaku zasshi* 32-6, June 1921. Hiraizumi edited the research papers of the Tōshōgū project members in 1927: HIRAIZUMI (ed.), *Tōshōgūshi*.

[56] See Florian NEUMANN 2011, *Politisches Denken im Japan des frühen 20. Jahrhunderts: Das Beispiel Uesugi Shinkichi*, 143 pp.

[57] *Higeki jūsō*, 60-61 / 318-319 / 326-327; WAKAI, *Hiraizumi*, 40-45. Ōkawa gave him his book *Indo ni okeru kokuminteki undō no genjō oyobi sono yurai* (»The present national movement in India and its origin«) that was prohibited from being published because of its anti-British content. (See Florian NEUMANN, ›Ōkawa Shūmei und der Weg zur „Shōwa-Erneuerung"‹, in *OAG Notizen*, 02/2015.)

[58] HIRAIZUMI, ›Ko Tanaka hakushi ikō no shuppan‹ (›Publishing the manuscripts of the late Dr. Tanaka‹), in *Shigaku zasshi* 33-12, December 1922.

[59] They had three sons: Hiraizumi Akira (1924-1995), Hiraizumi Hiroshi (1927-) and Hiraizumi Wataru (1929-2015).

[60] WAKAI, *Hiraizumi*, 47-54; *Higeki jūsō*, 327-328. He continued the *Azuma kagami* seminar into the 1930s.

[61] For Ludwig Riess in Japan see *Japanese Historians and the National Myths*, 73-80.

[62] HIRAIZUMI, ›Rekishi ni okeru jitsu to shin‹ (›Fact and Truth in history‹), in *Shigaku zasshi* 36-5, May 1925. (HIRAIZUMI 1926, *Waga rekishikan*, 344-380.) HIRAIZUMI, ›Rekishi wo ika ni manabu beki ka‹ (›How to study history?‹), in *Rekishi kyōiku*, October 1925.

[63] Croce wrote his book 1915 originally in German, *Zur Theorie und Geschichte der Historiographie*, followed by the Italian version *Teoria E Story Della Storiografia* in 1917. Hani finished his translation under the title *Rekishi no riron to rekishi* in 1926, for which Hiraizumi wrote a positive review in the journal *Shigaku zasshi* 37-12, December 1926.

⁶⁴ HIRAIZUMI, ›Rekishi ni okeru jitsu to shin‹, in HIRAIZUMI, *Waga rekishikan*, 379-380.

⁶⁵ HIRAIZUMI, ›Gendai rekishikan‹ (›The modern view of history‹), in *Taiyō* 32-1, January 1926. He renamed the article to ›*Waga rekishikan*‹ (›My view about history‹) for his following book with the same title.

⁶⁶ HIRAIZUMI 1926, *Chūsei ni okeru seishin seikatsu*, Tokyo: Shibundō.

⁶⁷ HIRAIZUMI 1926, *Waga rekishikan*. The volume contains his following articles: (1) ›*Waga rekishikan*‹; (2) ›*Ayamararetaru Nikkōbyō*‹, first published in *Shigaku zasshi* 32-2, February 1921;(3) ›*Yoritomo to nengō*‹, in *Shigaku zasshi* 28-10, October 1917; (4) ›*Za kanken*‹, in *Shigaku zasshi* 28-12, December 1917; (5) ›*Futatabi za ni tsuite guken wo tsugu*‹, in *Shigaku zasshi* 29-3, March 1918; (6) ›*Kameyama jōkō junkoku no gokigan*‹ (›Kameyama's prayer for the country‹), in *Shigaku zasshi* 31-12, December 1920; (7) ›*Ben no sōshi kō*‹, (›Thoughts on the Buddhist text volume *Ben no sōshi*‹), in *Rekishi chiri* 37-1, January 1921; (8) ›*Tokugawa Ieyasu no ikin*‹, in *Shigaku zasshi* 32-6, June 1921; (9) ›*Tōshō daigongen engi kō*‹ (›Thoughts on the *Tōshō daigongen engi*‹), in *Kokka* 32-1, July 1921; (10) ›*Shijō ni enmetsu seshi Itsutsuji no miya*‹, in *Taiyō* 28-11, September 1922; (11) ›*Shugo jitō ni kansuru shinsetsu no konponteki gobyū*‹ (›The systematic error in the new interpretation regarding the *shugo* and *jitō*‹), in *Shigaku zasshi* 34-1, January 1923; (12) ›*Ensei shijin Renzen*‹ (›Renzen, the poet who rejected the world‹), in *Bukkyōgaku* 2-5, May 1925; (13) ›*Rekishi ni okeru jitsu to shin*‹.

⁶⁸ HIRAIZUMI, ›Keiranshū yōshū to chūsei no shūkyō shisō‹ (›*Keiranshū yōshū* and religious thought in the Middle Ages‹) in *Shigaku zasshi* 37-6, June 1926.

⁶⁹ In 1920 the Imperial universities introduced the possibility to grant the doctor title for a written thesis valued by professional peers. In the field of Japanese history Hiraizumi was the first to receive the title in 1926 according to this new rule.

⁷⁰ UEDA, *Hiraizumi Kiyoshi*, 101-103.

⁷¹ See Brij TANKHA 2006, *Kita Ikki and the Making of Modern Japan*; George M. WILSON 1969, *Radical Nationalist in Japan: Kita Ikki, 1883—1937*.

⁷² Brian J. McVEIGH 2003, *Nationalisms of Japan: Managing and Mystifying Identity*, 52.

⁷³ HIRAIZUMI ›Rekishi no kaiko to kakushin no chikara‹ (›Reflecting on history and the power of renewal‹), in *Rekishi chiri*, October 1926. (HIRAIZUMI, *Kokushigaku no kotsuzui*, 18-29.)

⁷⁴ See Ōkawa's letters to Hiraizumi (29 Aug. and 22 Oct. 1927) in Ōkawa Shūmei kankei monjo kankōkai 1998, *Ōkawa Shūmei kankei monjo*, 449-450. For Ōkawa and Hiraizumi see SEIKE Motoyoshi 1995, *Senzen Shōwa nashonarizumu no shomondai*; NEUMANN, ›Ōkawa Shūmei und der Weg zur „Shōwa-Erneuerung"‹.

93

⁷⁵ HIRAIZUMI, ›*Kokushigaku no kotsuzui*‹ in *Shigaku zasshi* 38-8, August 1927. (HIRAIZUMI, *Kokushigaku no kotsuzui*, 1-17.) Hani dismissed Hiraizumi's thesis: HANI Gorō, ›*Hanrekishishugi hihan*‹ (›Criticizing Anti-Historicism‹), in *Shigaku zasshi* 39-6, June 1928.

⁷⁶ HIRAIZUMI, ›*Shinbutsu kankei no gyakuten*‹ (›The reversal in the relationship between the Gods and Buddha‹), in *Rekishi kyōiku*, April 1927. In January 1928, Ōkawa printed in his »Monthly Journal *Nippon*« (*Gekkan Nippon*) a thematic similar article by Hiraizumi: ›*Shinbutsu bunri no igi*‹ (›The meaning of Shintō's separation from Buddhism‹).

⁷⁷ HIRAIZUMI, ›*Nihon seishin hatten no dankai*‹ (›The developing stages of the Japanese Spirit‹), in *Shigaku zasshi* 39-4, April 1928. Already in his article ›*Shijō ni enmetsu seshi Itsutsuji no miya*‹ (›The Itsutsuji family that was erased from history‹) in September 1922 he saw history as everlasting and constant, while culture or state could be of temporary existence. Contrasting an 'eternal national essence' against the reality of cultural flux is a common theme within Japanese *kokutai* ideologues. See Florian NEUMANN, ›Die „*kokutai*-Wissenschaft" von Satomi Kishio (1897-1974)‹, in *OAG Notizen* 02/2014.

⁷⁸ HIRAIZUMI, ›*Nihon seishin hatten no dankai*‹, cited in UEDA, *Hiraizumi*, 97.

⁷⁹ UEDA, *Hiraizumi*, 98-99; HIRAIZUMI, ›*Chūsei bunka no kichō*‹ (›The keynote of medieval culture‹), in *Shirin* 14-1, January 1929; HIRAIZUMI, ›*Asuka jidai no bunka*‹ (›The culture of the Asuka period‹), in *Bukkyō bijutsu*, June 1929; HIRAIZUMI, ›*Nihon bunkashi ro gairon*‹ (›An overview of Japan's cultural history‹), in *Toyama kyōiku*, September 1929; HIRAIZUMI, ›*Kōza: Nihon bunka no hatten*‹ (›The development of Japanese culture‹), in *Gakkō kyōiku*, Nov./Dec. 1929. In 1928, he also wrote a short children's book on the Japanese Middle Ages (*Nihon jidō bunko 2—Nihon rekishi monogatari—chū*) as part of the series *Nihon jidō bunko* (»The Japanese Children's Library«) of the publisher Arusu (ARS) that comprised altogether 76 volumes from 1928 to 1930. In the summer of 1929, Hiraizumi edited the manuscript collection of the poet Ōe no Masafusa (1041-1111) that had been discovered in a temple in Mito a year before: HIRAIZUMI (ed.), *Gōto Tokudō gengan monshū*. His explanatory text ›*Gōto tokudō gengan monshū hakkan to yurai*‹ (›Publication and origin of the *Gōto Tokudō* collection‹) was also printed in HIRAIZUMI, *Kokushigaku no kotsuzui*, 194-241.

⁸⁰ Cited in WAKAI, *Hiraizumi*, 96-98.

⁸¹ KAMEI-DYCHE, ›An Engagement with the Scholarship on Mitogaku, from the 1930s to the Present‹, 77-78; YOSHIDA Toshizumi 1986, *Kōki Mitogaku kenkyū josetsu: Meiji Ishinshi no saikentō* (Tōkyō: Honpō Shoseki), 236-241. See also YOSHIDA Toshizumi 2003, *Mitogaku to Meiji ishin*.

94

⁸² HIRAIZUMI, ›*Kuriyama Senpō to Tani Jinzan*‹, in HIRAIZUMI, *Kokushigaku no kotsuzui*, 157-171. Tani published the notes he had made during Kuriyama's lectures: *Hōken taiki uchigiki.*

⁸³ HIRAIZUMI, ›*Kokka goji no seishin*‹ (›The spirit that protects our state‹), in *Kokushigaku no kotsuzui*, 146-156.

⁸⁴ HIRAIZUMI, ›*Kokushi wo tsuranuku meimei no chikara*‹, in *Kokushigaku no kotsuzui*, 39.

⁸⁵ HIRAIZUMI ›*Ichi no seishin wo kaku*‹ (›The one spirit that's missing‹), in *Kyōiku kenkyū*, January 1929, also in *Kokushigaku no kotsuzui*, 140-145.

⁸⁶ *Higeki jūsō*, 329. HIRAIZUMI, ›*Hashimoto Sanai sensei to sono shūhen*‹, in HIRAIZUMI 1933, *Bushidō no fukkatsu*, 43-57. Hiraizumi had already met Prince Chichibu in 1927.

⁸⁷ *Higeki jūsō*, 329-330; WAKAI, *Hiraizumi*, 193.

⁸⁸ HIRAIZUMI, ›*Nihon seishin*‹, in *Kokushigaku no kotsuzui*, 242-268.

⁸⁹ *Higeki jūsō*, 332-337.

⁹⁰ He later cited Reimann's work: Arnold REIMANN (ed.) 1928, *Geschichtswerk für höhere Schulen, Vol. 9: Kurt Gerstenberg, Ernst Krüger: Die Zeit von 1815 bis zur Gegenwart für die Oberstufe* (München/Berlin: Oldenbourg). See HIRAIZUMI, ›*Doitsu no rekishi kyōiku*‹ (›History education in Germany‹), in *Rekishi kyōiku*, April 1932. (HIRAIZUMI, *Bushidō no fukkatsu*, 58-92.)

⁹¹ UEMURA Kazuhide 2004, *Maruyama Masao to Hiraizumi* Kiyoshi, 302-303; Friedrich MEINECKE, ›Geschichte und Gegenwart‹ (1930/1939), in MEINECKE 1965, *Zur Theorie und Philosophie der Geschichte, Werke Vol. IV*, 94.

⁹² MEINECKE, ›Kausalitäten und Werte in der Geschichte‹, in *Historische Zeitschrift* 137, H. 1 1928, 25-26.

⁹³ *Higeki jūsō*, 338-349; UEDA, *Hiraizumi*, 119-127. He wrote three articles on the concepts *liberté, égalité* and *fraternité* and four essays introducing the French conservative writers Paul Bourget, Honoré de Balzac (1799-1850), Fréderic Le Play (1806-1882) and Hippolyte Taine (1828-1893). The latter four texts are included in his book *Dentō* (»Tradition«) which came out in 1940.

⁹⁴ *Higeki jūsō*, 47-50 / 61-62 / 349-361; UEDA, *Hiraizumi*, 128-132.

2. 'Times of National Emergency', the 1930s

[95] *Higeki jūsō*, 379. In November 1931 Hiraizumi wrote an essay about the Dominican friar Girolamo Savonarola (1452-1498) for whom he had shown an interest during his trip to Florence. He compared Savonarola, who had advocated a Christian renewal, with the Japanese Buddhist monk Nichiren (1222-1282): HIRAIZUMI, ›Sabonarora to Nichiren‹, in *Risshō bunka*, July 1932. (*Bushidō no fukkatsu*, 264-291.)

[96] *Higeki jūsō*, 378-379 / 383; WAKAI, *Hiraizumi*, 194-195. Katō Kanji presided over the *Keigakukai* until his death in 1939. The society was then led by Okada and afterwards by Lieutenant General Kaba Atsushi (1879-1960).

[97] *Higeki jūsō*, 379-382.

[98] For Chichibu's contacts with right-wing *coup* plotters see Ben-Ami SHILLONY 1973, *Revolt in Japan: The Young Officers and the February 26*, 96-102 / 106.

[99] The name *Society of Seven Lives* referred to Kusunoki. See NEUMANN, *Politisches Denken im Japan des frühen 20. Jahrhunderts: Das Beispiel Uesugi Shinkichi (1878-1929)*, 222-223 / 244 pp.

[100] The *Shukōkai* organized study sessions on the spiritual paragons that Hiraizumi revered: (1) Yamazaki Ansai and the *Kimon* school; (2) the *Jinnō shōtōki* and the *Mito* program *Shinron* (»A New Thesis«) by Aizawa Yasushi (1781-1863); (3) the *Meiji Constitution* as the Emperor's "political guiding document." In the 1930s, the *Shukōkai* became the largest right-wing student group at Tōkyō Imperial University. (TACHIBANA Takashi 2005, *Tennō to Tōdai*, vol. 2, 219-220; UEDA, *Hiraizumi*, 150-151.)

[101] Hiraizumi wrote about his time in the German town Göttingen where he had been well received by faculty students: HIRAIZUMI, ›Gechingen no omoide‹, in *Gekkan Nihon*, Feb. 1932. (*Bushidō no fukkatsu*, 93-112.)

[102] The Foreign Affairs Association of Japan 1938, *Politics and Political Parties in Japan*, 38.

[103] When Ōkawa was out of jail on bail waiting for his final sentence, Hiraizumi came to one of his gatherings on 20 July 1935. Ōkawa mentioned Hiraizumi in his prison diary on 20 August 1936—he compared him favorably to Hashimoto Keigaku. (HIROSE Shigemi, ›Hiraizumi Kiyoshi sensei to Ōkawa Shūmei hakase‹, in *Nihon*, October/November 2007; Ōkawa Shūmei kenshōkai 1986, *Ōkawa Shūmei nikki*, 159; WAKAI, *Hiraizumi*, 178-179.)

[104] He drafted a three-part essay on Burke's concerns about the French Revolution: HIRAIZUMI, ›Eikokumin no hankakumei seishin‹ (›The anti-revolutionary spirit of the British people‹), in *Rekishi chiri*, February to April 1932. A revised version titled ›Kakumei to Bāku‹ (›The Revolution and Burke‹) was printed in his book *Bushidō no fukkatsu*, 113-205. After the war, he republished his texts on Burke and the four French traditionalists in one volume: HIRAIZUMI 1964, *Kakumei to dentō* (»Revolution and Tradition«).

[105] *Higeki jūsō*, 405-407; UEDA, *Hiraizumi*, 142-143.

[106] HIRAIZUMI, ›Ishin no genri‹ (›The renewal principle‹), speech at the educational association *Shinbi dōshikai*, July 1932. (HIRAIZUMI, *Bushidō no fukkatsu*, 346-387.)

[107] YAMAZAKI Ansai et al., *Kōyūsō furoku* in NISHI, ABE, MARUYAMA, *Nihon shisō taikei 31: Yamazaki Ansai gakuha*, 200-243.

[108] *Higeki jūsō*, 383-390; WAKAI, *Hiraizumi*, 142.

[109] For differing positions in the *Kimon* tradition see OOMS, *Tokugawa Ideology*, 262 pp.

[110] HIRAIZUMI 1932, *Ansai sensei to Nihon seishin*, introduction.

[111] In 1934, *Nihon dōgaku engenroku* (»The Fountainhead of the Way of Learning in Japan«), a collection of *Kimon* texts originally collected in 1842, was reissued in eleven volumes by Oka Jirō (Oka Hyōson, 1864-1949) who also published several books about Yamazaki and his school. »The Complete works of Yamazaki Ansai« were published in five volumes by the »Academic Society for the Japanese Classics« (*Nihon koten gakkai*) in 1936 and 1937: *Yamazaki Ansai zenshū* (2 vols.) and *Zoku Yamazaki Ansai zenshū* (3 vols.).

[112] *Higeki jūsō*, 427-440; *Making History Matter*, 118.

[113] The book *Kokushigaku no kotsuzui* contains his following articles: (1) ›Kokushigaku no kotsuzui‹, first published in *Shigaku zasshi* 38-8, June 1927; (2) ›Rekishi no kaiko to kakushin no chikara‹, in *Rekishi chiri* 48-4, Sept. 1926; (3) ›Kokushi wo tsuranuku meimei no chikara‹, in *Yūshū* 183/184, February 1928; (4) ›Keiranshū yōshū to chūsei no shūkyō shisō‹, in *Shigaku zasshi* 37-6, May 1926; (5) ›Nihon seishin hatten no dankai‹, in *Shigaku zasshi* 39-4, March 1928; (6) ›Chūsei bunka no kichō‹, in *Shirin* 14-1, December 1928; (7) ›Ichi no seishin wo kaku‹, December 1928; (8) ›Kokka goji no seishin‹, November 1928; (9) ›Kuriyama Senpō to Tani Jinzan‹, in *Rekishi chiri* 3-10, January 1929; (10) ›Asuka jidai no bunku‹, in *Bukkyō bijutsu* 13, February 1929; (11) ›Gōto Tokudō gengan monshū hakkan to yurai‹, Sept. 1929; (12) ›Nihon seishin‹, March 1930.

[114]	HIRAIZUMI (ed.) 1933, *Jinnō shōtōki 1-4*; HIRAIZUMI & KOBAYASHI Kenzō (ed.) 1934, *Jinnō shōtōki*. Hiraizumi's explanatory texts — ›*Jinnō shōtōki no seiritsu*‹ (›How the *Jinnō shōtōki* came about‹) und ›*Jinnō shōtōki no naiyō*‹ (›The *Jinnō shōtōki*'s content‹) — are both in his book *Bushidō no fukkatsu*. He also wrote the chapter ›*Chūsei ni okeru kokutai kannen*‹ (›The *kokutai*-conception in the Japanese Middle Ages‹) for the Iwanami history series: Kokushi kenkyūkai 1933, *Iwanami kōza — Nihon no rekishi 4 chūsei* (Tōkyō: Iwanami Shoten).

[115]	Monbushō shakai kyōikukyoku (ed.) 1934, *Nihon shisō sōsho 10 — Jinnō shōtōki* (Tōkyō: Shakai Kyōikukai).

[116]	*Higeki jūsō*, 540.

[117]	WAKAI, *Hiraizumi*, 143-144.

[118]	*Kido Kōichi nikki*, cited in *Higeki jūsō*, 392-393; *Harada Kumao nikki*, cited in UEMURA Kazuhide 2004, *Maruyama Masao to Hiraizumi Kiyoshi*, 312; WAKAI, *Hiraizumi Kiyoshi*, 198-201; HARADA Kumao 1951, *Saionji Kinmochi to seikyoku 5*.

[119]	See the interview in 1978: ITŌ Takashi, ›*Tōkyō daigakushi kyūshokuin intabyū 3 — Hiraizumi Kiyoshi shi intabyū 5*‹, in *Tōkyō daigakushi kiyō 17*, March 1999, 122. Hiraizumi held a lecture before palace officials in December 1933 on Matsudaira Yoshitami's invitation: HIRAIZUMI, ›*Yoshida Shōin sensei*‹, in Kunaishō gojokai 1934, *Kōgū keisatsu kōen sokkiroku*.

[120]	*Kido Kōichi nikki*, cited in UEMURA Kazuhide 2010, *Shōwa no shisō*, 75; WAKAI, *Hiraizumi*, 204.

[121]	See Rekishigaku kenkyūkai (ed.) 1982, *Rekikyū hanseiki no ayumi* (Tōkyō: Aoki Shoten).

[122]	HIRAIZUMI, ›*Hashimoto Keigaku*‹, in *Kaizō*, January 1933. (*Bushidō no fukkatsu*, 11-42.)

[123]	*Higeki jūsō*, 400 pp.

[124]	*Ibid.*, 451 pp; WAKAI, *Hiraizumi*, 206.

[125]	Xie Fangde concluded that a devoted son, who respects his parents, certainly would be a loyal and supportive subject to the ruler: "The easiest way for a ruler to pick up a loyal subject or minister, … is to find him among the devoted sons in the country." (Cited in CHANG Chi-Yun 2012, *Confucianism: A Modern Interpretation*, 75.)

[126]	*Higeki jūsō*, 405. Hiraizumi's followers set up several small *Seiseijuku* branches, first in the Tōkyō area than in other cities. He named them all after phrases from Xie's poem: »Conifer Academy« (*Shōhakujuku*), »Academy of High Morality« (*Kōjōjuku*) etc.

[127]	*Higeki jūsō*, 407-413; UEDA, *Hiraizumi*, 145-146.

[128] The speech in September 1933 was used by the Ministry of Education as supplement material for school teachers: HIRAIZUMI 1934, *Shisō mondai shōgō 6—Kakumeiron*. (TATAMIYA, *Kami no kuni to chōrekishika*, 39.)

[129] HIRAIZUMI, ›Bushidō no fukkatsu‹ (›The revival of the Warrior's Creed‹), in *Dai'ajia shugi*, September 1933.

[130] Hiraizumi's book *Bushidō no fukkatsu* (»The Revival of the Warrior's Creed«) contains the articles: (1) ›Bushidō no fukkatsu‹; (2) ›Hashimoto Keigaku‹, in *Kaizō*, January 1933; (3) ›Hashimoto Sanai sensei to sono shūhen‹, first published in *Keigakukai kōenshū 2*, October 1929; (4) ›Doitsu no rekishi kyōiku‹, in *Rekishi kyōiku*, March /April 1932; (5) ›Gechingen no omoide‹, in *Gekkan Nihon*, February 1932; (6) ›Kakumei to Bāku‹, in *Rekishi chiri*, Feb./March/April 1932; (7) ›Jinnō shōtōki no seiritsu‹, in *Hakusanhon Jinnō shōtōki*, April 1933; (8) ›Jinnō shōtōki no naiyō‹, in *Hakusanhon Jinnō shōtōki*, April 1933; (9) ›Sabonarora to Nichiren‹, in *Risshō bunka*, July 1932; (10) ›Kōshitsu to kokumin dōtoku‹, in Higashi Fushimi no miya kazōban 1932, *Kōshitsushi no kenkyū*; (11) ›Ishin no genri‹, speech in July 1932.

[131] HIRAIZUMI, ›Bushidō no shinzui‹ (›The marrow of the Warrior's Creed‹), in Shinchōsha 1933, *Nippon seishin kōza 1*, 1-32. The first section of this essay was afterwards used in Middle Schools: Kōfūkan henshūsho 1935, *Chūgaku kokubun kyōkasho kyōju bikō maki 5*, 1-24.

[132] *Higeki jūsō*, 399-400 / 546.

[133] *Ibid.*, 414-415, 575-577. Rear Admiral Ueda Muneshige (1884-1939) called Hiraizumi to the *Navy Engineering College* again in October 1934 to continue his lecture visits there once a year.

[134] AGAWA Hiroyuki 1996, *Takamatsu no miya to kaigun*, noted in UEDA, *Hiraizumi*, 158.

[135] *Higeki jūsō*, 416-417; WAKAI, *Hiraizumi*, 209-210.

[136] *Higeki jūsō*, 422 / 470.

[137] *Katō Kanji nikki*, cited in *Higeki jūsō*, 570-571. Admiral Katō ended his military career in November 1935 and died in April 1939.

[138] *Higeki jūsō*, 582-609 / 627. Matsudaira Nagayoshi graduated from the Navy Engineering College in March 1937.

[139] *Ibid.*, 443. The *Kenmu Remembrance Committee* printed its report in August 1934: Kenmu no chūkō roppyakunen kinenkai (ed.), *Kenmu no chūkō roppyakunen kinenkai jigyō hōkoku*.

[140] *Making History Matter*, 238-239.

[141] HIRAIZUMI, ›Nihon chūkō‹, in Kenmu no chūkō roppyakunen kinenkai (ed.) 1934, *Kenmu no chūkō*.

[142] HIRAIZUMI 1934, *Kenmu chūkō no hongi*. He republished the book in 1983.

[143] *Ibid.*, 177 pp.

[144] *Ibid.*, 297 pp.

[145] HIRAIZUMI 1940, *Dentō*, 343-346.

[146] Hiraizumi privately distributed an expanded version of *Chū to gi* among his followers. A Chinese translation came out in the Japanese colony of Taiwan in 1942.

[147] *Higeki jūsō*, 142 / 449 / 575. The Army War College made his presentations into a textbook: HIRAIZUMI 1936, *Kokushi kōwa* (»Lectures about our National History«).

[148] HIRAIZUMI, *Kokushi kōwa*, 66.

[149] In an article he tried to prove the authenticity of the »Text from the Border Fortress« (*Kanjōsho*), that Kitabatake was said to have written in 1342 but that was widely considered a forgery: HIRAIZUMI, ›Kanjōsho bengo‹, (›Defending the *Kanjōsho*‹), in *Shigaku zasshi* 46-1, January 1935. See his later reflections on this topic in *Higeki jūsō*, 440-443.

[150] *Higeki jūsō*, 443.

[151] Hiraizumi wrote a booklet for the Minatogawa Shrine: HIRAIZUMI 1935, *Dainankō roppyakunensai wo mukaete*.

[152] Cited in MORRIS, *The Nobility of Failure*, 95.

[153] *Making History Matter*, 239.

[154] *Higeki jūsō*, 443 / 447.

[155] *Ibid.*, 447-449 / 575. His speeches in Korea (›Nihon seishin kōwa‹) were printed in Chōsen kyōikukai, *Bunkyō no Chōsen* 122, October 1935.

[156] HIRAIZUMI, ›Makoto no Nihonjin‹, in HIRAIZUMI, *Dentō*, 51-52. The text was first published in 1936 in Ōsaka as a booklet with the title ›Sakura sensei no seishin‹ (›The Spirit of Master Sakura‹). During the war Sakura was celebrated as a national role model.

[157] See NEUMANN, *Politisches Denken im Japan des frühen 20. Jahrhunderts: Das Beispiel Uesugi Shinkichi (1878-1929)*.

[158] See YAMAZAKI Masahiro 2017, *"Tennō kikan setsu" jiken*. To show his patriotism while under attack Minobe put his name under a large report about the Kusunoki celebrations in the *Kōbe Yūshin Nippō* newspaper on 25 May 1935.

[159] ›Kokutai meichō mondai saiseimei‹, in *Tōkyō Asahi Shinbun*, 16 October 1935; YAMAZAKI, *"Tennō kikan setsu" jiken*, 197-200.

[160] See KOYAMA Tsunemi 1989, *Tennō kikansetsu to kokumin kyōiku*; TAKANO Kunio 1989, *Tennōsei kokka no kyōikuron — kyōgaku sasshin hyōgikai no kenkyū*.

161 HIRAIZUMI 1977, *Nihon no higeki to risō*, 369-375. Hiraizumi didn't say much about his relationship with Uesugi, who also came from Fukui and shared his traditionalistic beliefs.

162 On 27 January 1936, Hiraizumi led a seminar at the Army Academy about "Kusunoki's loyal death as the formative spirit that inspired the Meiji Restoration." HIRAIZUMI, ›Meiji ishin no konpon seishin‹, in Rikugun shikan gakkō (ed.) 1937, *Nihon seishin kōenshū dai 2 shu* (Tōkyō: Rikugun Shikan Gakkō Kōtōkan Shūkaijo).

163 See SHILLONY, *Revolt in Japan: The Young Officers and the February 26, 1936 Incident*; Herbert P. BIX 2000, *Hirohito and the Making of Modern Japan*, 297 pp.

164 *Higeki jūsō*, 458-459.

165 *Kido Kōichi nikki*, 21 July 1932, cited in HATA Ikuhiko 1984, *Hirohito tennō itsutsu no ketsudan*, 36; SHILLONY, *Revolt in Japan: The Young Officers and the February 26*, 100.

166 *Higeki jūsō*, 380-381 / 458-459; TATAMIYA, *Kami no kuni to chōrekishika Hiraizumi Kiyoshi*, 18-45; WAKAI, *Hiraizumi*, 216-221.

167 Hirohito to Vice Chamberlain Hirohata Tadataka (1884-1961). *Kido Kōichi nikki*, 28 February 1936, cited in *Revolt in Japan: The Young Officers and the February 26*, 100; BIX, *Hirohito and the Making of Modern Japan*, 301.

168 IWATA Masataka, ›Misui ni owatta kirikomi keikaku (ni niroku jiken no shinjijitsu)‹, in *Chūō kōron*, March 1992, 320-329; WAKAI, *Hiraizumi*, 222-223. Iwata mistakenly noted that the meeting took place on the evening of February 27th.

169 In April 1936 Iwata was adopted by Major Ida Iwakusu (1881-1864) and then used the name Ida Masataka until 1955. Ida Iwakusu had a seat in the House of Peers and supported Kikuchi in his accusations against Minobe in 1935.

170 Tanaka Takashi collected Hiraizumi's papers related to the *February 26 Incident*: TANAKA Takashi 2012, *Hiraizumi shigaku no shinzui*, chapters 1-3.

171 *Kami no kuni to chōrekishika Hiraizumi Kiyoshi*, 36-37. In early April 1936, Hiraizumi spoke on NHK radio about the *Jinnō shōtōki*: HIRAIZUMI, ›Jinnō shōtōki kōwa‹, NHK Radio talk, 1-4 April 1936, in *Dentō*, 119-148. On 27 April 1936, he made a presentation about the *Jinnō shōtōki* at the »Technical Research Center of the Navy« (*kaigun gijutsu kenkyūjo*).

172 Hiraizumi came to the Navy Engineering College in Nov. 1936, May 1937, Dec. 1938, March 1941, June 1942, June 1943 and Sept. 1943. (*Higeki jūsō*, 575-577; UEDA, *Hiraizumi*, 159.)

173 WAKAI, *Hiraizumi*, 225-227; UEDA, *Hiraizumi*, 166.

174 *Takamatsu no miya nikki*, 27 May 1937, cited in WAKAI, *Hiraizumi*, 225-227, UEDA, *Hiraizumi*, 166.

3. The Road into War, 1937-1941

[175] *Making History Matter*, 241-242. Nagoya und Matsumoto edited the journal *Kenmu* until the end of the Second World War. They later wrote several books on the *Mito School*, for example: NAGOYA Tokimasa 1986, *Shinpan—Mito Mitsukuni*.

[176] HIRAIZUMI 1936, *Banbutsu ruten*, 1.

[177] *Banbutsu ruten*, 166.

[178] *Ibid.*, 219.

[179] *Ibid.*, 256-257.

[180] He gave the lecture ›*Eien no seimei*‹ on 13 November 1936 at the Ōsaka Police Headquarters: Ōsakafu keisatsubu keimuka 1937, *Nippon seishin dainihen* (»Second Volume on the Japanese Spirit«).

[181] Hiraizumi stressed Maki's argument throughout the war. In 1964 he presided over the 100th anniversary of Maki's death: HIRAIZUMI, ›*Maki Izumi no kami—Nanshiron gigi*‹ (›An analysis of Maki's commentary *Nanshiron*‹), in HIRAIZUMI 1972, *Sentetsu wo aogu*, chapter 19.

[182] See MORRIS, *The Nobility of Failure*, 92-94.

[183] WAKAI, *Hiraizumi*, 186-190. Hiraizumi visited the *Sondōkan* again in April 1937.

[184] HIRAIZUMI, *Nihon no higeki to risō*, 45-46; *Higeki jūsō*, 470-471.

[185] *Nihon no higeki to risō*, 184-185; WAKAI, *Hiraizumi*, 227-228.

[186] Konoe only added the word 'extraordinary' (*hanahada*) to Hiraizumi's draft. (*Nihon no higeki to risō*, 185-188; HIRAIZUMI 2005, *Sanga ari*, 308-314; KUDŌ Miyoko 2006, *Ware Sugamo ni shutto sezu*, 148. See also YAGAMI Kazuo 2006, *Konoe Fumimaro and the Failure of Peace in Japan, 1937-1941*, 39.)

[187] WAKAI, *Hiraizumi*, 235.

[188] *Ibid.*, 234; *Kami no kuni to chōrekishika Hiraizumi Kiyoshi*, 36; FURUKAWA Takahisa 2005, *Shōwa senchūki no gikai to gyōsei*. They ringleaders of the *February 26 Incident* were executed in the summer of 1937 together with the civilians Kita and Nishida. (*Revolt in Japan*, 198 pp.)

[189] Nihon bunka kyōkai (ed.) 1937, *Kyōgaku sasshin hyōgikai tōshin oyobi kengi*.

[190] See HALL, Robert King (ed.) / GAUNTLETT, John Owen 1949, *Kokutai no Hongi—Cardinal Principles of the National Entity of Japan.*

[191] SHISHIDA Fumiaki, ›Kenkoku daigaku no kyōiku to Ishiwara Kanji‹, in *Waseda daigaku ningen kagaku kenkyū* 6-1, 1993, 109-123; *Higeki jūsō*, 469 pp.

[192] *Higeki jūsō*, 469-472.

[193] *Ibid.*, 473-475; WAKAI, *Hiraizumi*, 229-232. Teaching courses at *Manchu State Building University* began in May 1938. On the basis of Manchukuo's official creed as a nation of 'Five Races Under One Union' (*gozoku kyōwa*), the students were of Chinese, Manchu, Japanese, Mongolian and Korean ethnicity with a few Russians enrolled as well. The university was controlled by the *Guandong*-Army. The titular rector was the Manchurian prime minister Zhang Jinghui (1871-1959) but the administration was done by the vice rector, to which Sakuta Shōichi was appointed in January 1939. (MIURA Hideyuki 2017, *Goshiki no niji—Manshū kenkoku daigaku sotsugyōseitachi no sengo*; KOBAYASHI Kinzō 2002, *Hakutō—Manshūkoku kenkoku daigaku.*)

[194] WAKAI, *Hiraizumi*, 136-141. The notes for Hiraizumi's lectures on *Japanese Thought History* from 1938 until 1945 were published in his journal *Geirin*: ›Hiraizumi Kiyoshi kyōju 'Nihon shisōshi' kōgi nōto‹, in *Geirin*, April 2002 to October 2007.

[195] HIRAIZUMI / TERADA (ed.) 1938, *Ōhashi Totsuan sensei zenshū*, vol 1. (The Second and Third volume came out in February 1939 and July 1943.) Terada initially studied East Asian History (*tōyōshi*) but voiced his discontent over the department's lectures and graduated with a biography about Ōhashi (TERADA Takeshi 1936, *Ōhashi Totsuan sensei den*). For being a vocal *Shukōkai* activist, Hiraizumi recommended him for the position of vice assistant in the Shintō Studies Department (*Shintōgaku kenkyūshitsu*) before he assigned him to the *Manchu State Building University*, where he led one of the university's dormitories and was feared for his discipline. In 1945 Terada was interned by the Soviets in Siberia and returned to Japan in 1956 to become a professor at »Asia University« (*Ajia daigaku*) in Tōkyō. (SHISHIDA Fumiaki 2003, *Manshūkoku Kenkoku daigaku ni okeru budō kyōiku*, 142.)

[196] Yūzankaku 1938, *Nihongaku sōsho 4—Bukyō honron, Bukyō shōgaku, Bukyō zensho kōroku*; Yūzankaku 1938, *Nihongaku sōsho 8—Seimeiron, Kyūmon ihan, Kōdōkan kijutsugi*; Yūzankaku 1938, *Nihongaku sōsho 2—Hōken taiki, Hōken taiki uchigi*.

[197] NAKAMURA Kōya 1934, *Kenmu no chūkō no kaiko* (Shōkasha); NAKAMURA Kōya 1935, *Zō shōichi'i Tachibana ason Masashige den* (Dainankō ryoppyakunen taisai hōsankai); NAKAMURA Kōya 1935, *Kokubō to Nihon seishin* (Saitamaken kokubō gikai).

¹⁹⁸ ABE Takeshi 1999, *Taiheiyō sensō to rekishigaku*, 62-67; WAKAI, *Hiraizumi*, 162-163. In May 1938, Hiraizumi spoke about Nitta at the Fujishima Shrine *(Fujishima jinja)* in Fukui — one of the Fifteen Shrines of the *Kenmu* Restoration — that was broadcasted on radio: HIRAIZUMI, ›*Nitta Yoshisada kō wo shinobu*‹ (›In memory of Nitta Yoshisada‹), in *Dentō*, 278-341. See also HIRAIZUMI 1938, *Kitabatake Akiie kō wo shinobu* (›In memory of *Kitabatake Akiie*‹), Ōsakafu Shakai Kyōikuka; HIRAIZUMI, ›*Kitabatake Akiie Nitta Yoshisada ryōkō wo shinobu*‹, in *Kenmu* 3/4, July 1938.

¹⁹⁹ Cited in WAKAI, *Hiraizumi*, 137. Maruyama became an assistant in the Department for Political Science *(seijigaku)* in 1937 and focused his research on political thought. See MARUYAMA Masao 1974, *Studies in the Intellectual History of Tokugawa Japan*. For his work on the Ansai School see MARUYAMA Masao 1980 ›*Ansaigaku to Ansai gakuha*‹ in NISHI, ABE, MARUYAMA, *Nihon shisō taikei 31: Yamazaki Ansai gakuha*, 601-674.

²⁰⁰ *Higeki jūsō*, 478-485. He made a speech in Kagoshima: HIRAIZUMI, ›*Hijōji ni odoru Yamato damashii*‹ (›The Yamato Spirit that vibrates in the time of emergency‹), in *Kagoshima Shinbun*, 12-23 July 1938.

²⁰¹ See Rana MITTER 2013, *China's War with Japan, 1937-1945*, 141 pp.

²⁰² 'The Imperial Military Reservist Association' *(teikoku zaigō gunjinkai)* appointed Hiraizumi to the role of 'adviser' and printed his lecture in its journal *Kenyū*: HIRAIZUMI, ›*Kokushi no ganmoku*‹ (›The Essence of Japan's History‹), in *Kenyū* 32/7-11, July to Nov. 1938. Also published in HIRAIZUMI 1943, *Tenpei ni teki nashi*, 147-405.

²⁰³ *Ibid.* He elaborated on his concept of 'true science' in two seminars at the Army Academy in June 1937: HIRAIZUMI, ›*Shinjitsu no gakumon*‹, in Rikugun shikan gakkō 1937, *Nihon seishin kōenshū*.

²⁰⁴ *Tenpei ni teki nashi*, 342-349.

²⁰⁵ *Ibid.*, 349.

²⁰⁶ HIRAIZUMI, ›*Dainihonshi*‹ (›The History of Great Japan‹), in Naimushō keihōkyoku 1939, *Keisatsu kanbu Yokuonkan kōwaroku*.

²⁰⁷ WAKAI, *Hiraizumi*, 236.

²⁰⁸ HIRAIZUMI, ›*Dainihonshi*‹.

²⁰⁹ See Edwin B. LEE, ›Nichiren and Nationalism: The Religious Patriotism of Tanaka Chigaku‹, in *Monumenta Nipponica* 30/1, Spring 1975, 19-35. Tanaka's *kokutai* exegesis was further developed by his son Satomi Kishio who wrote a vast array of books proclaiming a '*kokutai* science' *(kokutai kagaku)*. See NEUMANN, ›Die „*kokutai*-Wissenschaft" von Satomi Kishio (1897-1974)‹, 25-50.

²¹⁰ INOUE Tetsujirō / UEDA Kazutoshi (ed.) / HIRAIZUMI (commentary) 1934, *Nihon shoki — Dainihon bunko kokushihen*.

²¹¹ HIRAIZUMI, *Hakkō ichiu*, booklet printed by the Reservist Association in March 1939.

²¹² *Higeki jūsō*, 503-504; HIRAIZUMI 1939, *Kokutai shikan ni motozuku Nihon gaikōshi* ("A chronicle of Japan's Foreign Policy based on the *kokutai* view of history"), Tōkyō: *Gaimushō shūyō tanren shiryō 1*, July 1939.

²¹³ *Higeki jūsō*, 529-530.

²¹⁴ Kenneth RUOFF 2010, *Imperial Japan at its Zenith: The Wartime Celebration of the Empire's 2,600th Anniversary*, 40. For the 'Commission of Inquiry into Historical Sites Related to Emperor Jinmu' (*Jinmu tennō seiseki chōsa iinkai*), formed by the Ministry of Education in 1938, see *Japanese Historians and the National Myths, 1600-1945*, 180 pp.

²¹⁵ WAKAI, *Hiraizumi*, 149-152.

²¹⁶ Kido and Hiraizumi met privately three weeks after the Gotoba event. See *Higeki jūsō*, 497-502; HIRAIZUMI, ›Gotoba tennō nanahyakunen Godaigo tennō roppyakunen no onsai wo mukae tatematsurite‹ (›Awaiting the 700th and 600th death anniversaries of Gotoba and Godaigo‹), in *Kenmu* 4-1, January 1939; HIRAIZUMI, ›Gotoba tennō wo shinobitematsuru‹ (›Commemorating Emperor Gotoba‹), March 1939, in HIRAIZUMI 2014, *Hiraizumi Kiyoshi hakase shintō ronshō*, 198-223.

²¹⁷ *Higeki jūsō*, 486-493. On his way to Kyūshū, Hiraizumi spoke at a school in Ōsaka about "Gotoba's wish to reestablish Japan in its right form as the moral country (*dōgi no kuni*)." His travel report ›Mera no sakura‹ (›The cherry flowers in Mera‹) appeared later in the weekly journal *Shūkan Asahi*, 19 April 1942, and also in his book *Tenpei ni teki nashi*, 29 pp.

²¹⁸ *Higeki jūsō*, 530-532. The Commission submitted its final report in March 1942: Monbushō shūkyōkyoku hozonka 1942, *Jinmu tennō seiseki chōsa hōkoku*.

²¹⁹ RUOFF, *Imperial Japan at its Zenith: The Wartime Celebration of the Empire's 2,600th Anniversary*, 40.

²²⁰ Kenmu gikai 1939, *Godaigo tennō hōsan ronbunshū* (»A Collection of Eulogies for Emperor Godaigo«); *Higeki jūsō*, 503 pp. See also his speech from March 1940: HIRAIZUMI, ›Godaigo tennō no seitoku wo aogitatematsuru‹ (›Looking up to Godaigo's sacred virtue‹), in *Hiraizumi Kiyoshi hakase shintō ronshō*, 254-282.

²²¹ HIRAIZUMI, ›Kōa no gendōryoku‹ (›The principal force that's propelling Asia‹), in Daidō gakuin 1940, *Ronsō daini shū* (Shinkyō: Daidō Gakuin).

²²² The book *Dentō* consisted of: (1) ›Makoto no Nihonjin‹ (written in November 1935); (2) ›Bukyō shōgaku kōwa‹ (originally titled ›Bushidō‹, NHK series, 2-9 November 1939); (3) ›Jinnō shōtōki kōwa‹ (NHK series, 1-4 April 1936); (4) ›Gukanshō to Jinnō shōtōki‹ (*Shigaku zasshi* 47-9, September 1936); (5) ›Kanjōsho bengo‹ (*Shigaku zasshi* 46-1, January 1935); (6) ›Nitta Yoshisada kō wo shinobu‹ (speech at Fukujima Shrine, May 1938). The volume's second half comprised his biographic articles: (6) ›Balzac‹; (7) ›Le Play‹; (8) ›Taine‹ and (9) ›Bourget‹.

[223] *Higeki jūsō*, 524-528; UEDA, *Hiraizumi*, 183 pp. Hiraizumi noted how Pu Yi asked him questions and invited him for a cup of tea. He called the Manchurian Emperor 'wise' (*sōmei*) to follow his advice. Afterwards, Hiraizumi delivered a speech at the *Manchu State Building University* and then travelled with staff officers to occupied Beiping.

[224] *Imperial Japan at its Zenith*, 60. A »State Foundation Shintō-Mausoleum« (*Kenkoku shinbyō*) for the Japanese Sun-Goddess was built on the palace ground in Xinjing, where Pu Yi performed the initiation rites on July 15th 1940.

[225] HIRAIZUMI 1940, *Kenmu no chūkō ni tsuite*, published by the Japanese Foreign Ministry.

[226] *Higeki jūsō*, 547-548.

[227] *Ibid.*, 548-551.

[228] For Konoe's speech ›*Taimei wo haishite*‹ (›The Imperial order has been given‹) and Hiraizumi's initial draft, see KONOE Fumimaro 1940, *Senjika no kokumin ni okeru Konoe shushō ensetsushū*, 159 pp; *Higeki jūsō*, 549 pp.

[229] Slightly adjusted quote from ITŌ, *Commentaries on the Constitution of the Empire of Japan*, XI; JANSEN, *The Making of Modern Japan*, 395.

[230] ITŌ, *Commentaries on the Constitution of the Empire of Japan*, 153-154.

[231] See NEUMANN, *Politisches Denken im Japan des frühen 20. Jahrhunderts*.

[232] *Higeki jūsō*, 554.

[233] Gordon M. BERGER 1977, *Parties Out of Power in Japan, 1931–1941*, 267-268; HORI Yukio 1997, *Senzen no kokkashugi undōshi*, 382 pp.

[234] *Higeki jūsō*, 552-555.

[235] *Ibid.*, 523/556; *Imperial Japan at its Zenith*, 15-17. Hiraizumi made a speech on 26 February 1940 in Nagoya: HIRAIZUMI 1941, *Kigen nisen roppyakunen wo mukaete* (»The coming founding year 2600«), Nagoya: Nagoyashi Shakai Kyōikuka. He also wrote a booklet for the *Hakusan Shrine* in Fukui: HIRAIZUMI 1940, *Kigen nisen roppyakunen wo mukaete Jinnō shōtōki wo omou* (»Thoughts about the *Jinnō shōtōki* at the founding year 2600«), Fukui: Hakusan Jinja.

[236] HIRAIZUMI, ›*Kenmu chūkō to rekishi no shinzui*‹ (›The *Kenmu* restoration and the essence of history‹), in KANOKOGI Kazunobu 1941, *Kōkokugaku taikō*. Cited in *Higeki jūsō*, 423-424.

[237] *Higeki jūsō*, 610.

[238] *Ibid.*, 577-578. Rear Admiral Tokunaga visited Hiraizumi in July 1941 with his intent to resume his lecture courses.

[239] *Ibid.*, 149-150.

[240] *Ibid.*, 148-155.

Glossary

Aa chūshin Nanshi no haka
　嗚呼忠臣楠子之墓

Aizawa Yasushi　會澤安

Akihito　明仁

Amaterasu Ōmikami　天照大神

Ame no Oshihomimi　天忍穂耳尊

Anami Korechika　阿南惟幾

Andō Nobumasa　安藤信正

Ansei no taigoku　安政の大獄

Araki Sadao　荒木貞夫

Arima Ryōkitsu　有馬良橘

Asami Keisai　浅見絅斎

Ashikaga Takauji　足利尊氏

Azuma kagami　『吾妻鏡』

banbutsu ruten　萬物流轉

bi　美

bōkyō kyōtei　防共協定

Bōnanken　望楠軒

bukyō　武教

bunke　分家

bunmei kaika　文明開化

bushidō　武士道

Chiang Kaishek　蒋介石

Chichibu no miya Yasuhito
　秩父宮雍仁

Chihaya　千早

Chihayajō　千早城

chōkoku　肇國

chū　忠

chūkō　忠孝

chūsei　中世

chūsei kōgi　中世講義

chūshi　忠死

chūshin　忠臣

Dai'ajia kyōkai　大亞細亞協會

daigo shidan　第五師團

Daigo Tennō　醍醐天皇

dai'ichi kōkū kantai　第一航空艦隊

dai'ichi shidan　第一師團

109

dai jūichi shidan 第十一師團

daimyō 大名

Dainihonshi 『大日本史』

Dainihon teikoku kenpō
大日本帝國憲法

dairoku kantai 第六艦隊

daishi kōtō gakkō 第四高等學校

danshaku 男爵

Datong xueyuan / Daidō gakuin
大同學院

dō 道

Dōgen 道元

dōgi 道義

dōgi kokka no fukko
道義國家の復古

dōgi no kuni 道義の國

Echizen 越前

eien no seimei 永遠の生命

Eiheiji 永平寺

Enryakuji 延暦寺

Eshū 恵秀

Etajima 江田島

fueki no michi 不易の道

Fujii Naoaki 藤井直明

Fujishima jinja 藤島神社

Fujita Tōko 藤田東湖

Fujita Yūkoku 藤田幽谷

fukkatsu 復活

fukko 復古

Fukui 福井

Fukui-Echizen 福井越前

Fukui han 福井藩

Fukuikai 福井會

Fukui Kurabu 福井倶楽部

Geirin 『藝林』

Gekkan Nihon 『月刊日本』

gendai 現代

genjōin 玄成院

Genkō no ran 元弘の亂

genrō 元老

Genyōsha 玄洋社

gi 義

Godaigo Tennō 後醍醐天皇

goichigo jiken 五・一五事件

Gomurakami Tennō 後村上天皇

Gotoba Tennō 後鳥羽天皇

gozoku kyōwa 五族協和

Guangwu 光武

Guomindang 國民黨

gyakushin 逆臣

haibutsu kishaku 廢佛毀釈

hakkō ichiu 八紘一宇

Hakusan 白山

Hakusan jinja 白山神社

Hamada Kunimatsu 濱田國松

hangyaku 反逆

Hani Gorō 羽仁五郎

hanran 叛亂

harakiri mondō 腹切り問答

Hara Takashi 原敬

Hashimoto Keigaku
(Hashimoto Sanai)
橋本景岳 （橋本左内）

Hatta Yūjirō 八田裕二郎

Hayashi Gahō 林鵞峯 Hayashi
Kentarō 林健太郎 Hayashi
Razan 林羅山 Hayashi Senjūrō
林銑十郎 *Heisenji* 平泉寺

Heisenji mura 平泉寺村

Higo 肥後

Hijikata Seibi 土方成美

hijōji 非常時

Hiraga shukugaku 平賀蕭學

Hiraga Yuzuru 平賀譲

Hiraizumi Akira 平泉洸

Hiraizumi Hayako 平泉逸子

Hiraizumi Hiroshi 平泉汪

Hiraizumi Katsugō 平泉恰合

Hiraizumi Kiyoshi 平泉澄

Hiraizumi Takafusa 平泉隆房

Hiraizumi Wataru 平泉渉

Hiranuma Kiichirō 平沼騏一郎

Hirata Atsutane 平田篤胤

Hirohata Tadataka 広幡忠隆

Hirohito 裕仁

Hirosaki 弘前

Hirota Kōki 廣田弘毅

Hōjō 北條

Hōken taiki 『保建大記』

Hōken taiki uchigiki
　『保建大記打聞』

Hokkaidō teikoku daigaku
　北海道帝國大學

hokuchō 北朝

Honchō tsugan 『本朝通鑑』

Honjō Shigeru 本庄繁

Ida Iwakusu 井田磐楠

Ii Naosuke 井伊直弼

Ikazuri jinja 坐摩神社

ikkō ikki 一向一揆

Inoue Shigeyoshi 井上成美

Inoue Tetsujirō 井上哲次郎

Inukai Tsuyoshi 犬養毅

Irokawa Daikichi 色川大吉

ishin 維新

Ishiwara Kanji 石原莞爾

Itagaki Seishirō 板垣征四郎

Itō Hirobumi 伊藤博文

Itō Takashi 伊藤隆

Iwata Masataka (Ida Masataka)
　岩田正孝 （井田正孝）

Izanami 伊弉冊尊

Jianwu 建武

Jingū Kōgō 神功皇后

Jinmukai 神武會

Jinmu Tennō 神武天皇

Jinmu tennō seiseki chōsa iinkai
神武天皇聖蹟調査委員會

Jinmu tennō sōgyō 神武天皇創業

Jinnō shōtōki 『神皇正統記』

jitsu 實

jitsugaku 實學

jiyū minken undō 自由民權運動

jōdai 上代

Jōkyū no ran 承久の亂

jōyu 上諭

jūgatsu jiken 十月事件

juku 塾

junsui 純粹

Kagawa 香川

kaigun daigakkō 海軍大學校

kaigun heigakkō 海軍兵學校

kaigun kikan gakkō 海軍機關學校

kaigunshō kyōikukyoku 海軍省教育局

kaigun Yūshūkai 海軍有終會

Kaizō 『改造』

Kakei Katsuhiko 筧克彦

kakumei 〔géming〕 革命

kakushin 革新

kakushin uyoku 革新右翼

Kaku Tomeo 加来止男

Kamiōsaki 上大崎

kamiyo 神代

Kanazawa 金澤

kannen uyoku 觀念右翼

Kanokogi Kazunobu 鹿子木員信

kantaiha 艦隊派

Kantōgun 關東軍

Karasaki Hitachinosuke
唐崎常陸介之

Kasumigaura kaigun kōkūtai
霞ヶ浦海軍航空隊

Katō Kanji 加藤寛治

Katorimaru 香取丸

Katsuyama 勝山

Katsuyama han 勝山藩

Kawachi 河內

Kawai Eijirō 河合榮治郎

Kawarada Kakichi 河原田稼吉

kazoku seido 家族制度

kei 敬

Keigakukai 景岳會

keiko 稽古

Keiranshū yōshū 『渓嵐拾葉集』

keiyakuha 契約派

Kekki shuisho 「蹶起趣意書」

kenkoku 建國

Kenkoku shinbyō 建國神廟

Kenmu 建武

Kenmu 『建武』

Kenmu chūko jūgosha
建武中興十五社

Kenmugikai 建武義會

Kenmu jinja 建武神社

Kenmu no chūkō 建武の中興

Kenmu no chūkō roppyakunen kinenkai
　建武の中興六百年記念會

kenpei shireibu 憲兵司令部

kenpō happu chokugo
　「憲法發布勅語」

kenpōgaku 憲法學

Kido Kōichi　木戸幸一

kigen nisen roppyakunen kinen
　紀元二千六百年記念

kigensetsu 紀元節

Kikuchishi kinnō kenshōkai
　菊池氏勤王顯彰會

Kikuchi Takefusa　菊池武房

Kikuchi Takemitsu　菊池武光

Kikuchi Takeo　菊池武夫

Kikuchi Taketoki　菊池武時

kimi / kun 君

Kimongaku 崎門學

kinki kakumei 錦旗革命

kinsei 近世

Kishi Nobusuke　岸信介

Kitabatake Akiie　北畠顯家

Kitabatake Chikafusa　北畠親房

Kita Ikki　北一輝

Kiyoura Keigo　清浦奎吾

kizoku'in 貴族院

kō 公

kōbu gattai 公武合體

Kōbun Tennō　弘文天皇

kodai 古代

kōdō 皇道

kōdōha 皇道派

Kōdōkan 弘道館

Kōdōkanki 『弘道館記』

Kojiki 『古事記』

Kōjōjuku 綱常塾

*kokka no shin'un wo fuchi semu
　koto wo nozomi*
　國家ノ進運ヲ扶持セムコトヲ望ミ

kokka shugi 國家主義

kōkoku 皇國

Kōkoku dōshikai　興國同志會

kōkoku no dōgi 皇國の道義

kokugaku 國學

kokumin seishin bunka kenkyūjo
　國民精神文化研究所

kokumin seishin sōdōin undō
　國民精神總動員運動

kokumu daijin 國務大臣

kokushi 國史

kokushi dai'ichi kōza 國史第一講座

kokushi daini kōza 國史第二講座

kokushi gakka 國史學科

kokutai 國體

kokutaigaku kōza 國體學講座

kokutai genriha 國體原理派

kokutai meichō seimei
　『國體明徵聲明』

Kokutai no hongi　『國體の本義』

Konoe Fumimaro　近衛文麿

Konoe hohei dai'ichi rentai
近衛歩兵第一聯隊

Kōno Shōzo 河野省三

Kōyūsō furoku 『拘幽操附録』

kōzō 構造

Kudan gunjin kaikan 九段軍人會館

Kujakuki 『孔雀記』

Kume Kunitake 久米邦武

kunai daijin 宮内大臣

kunaishō 宮内省

Kuriyama Senpō 栗山潛鋒

Kuroita Katsumi 黒板勝美

Kuromaru 黒丸

Kusunoki Magosaburō 楠木孫三郎

Kusunoki Masashige 楠木正成

Kusunoki Masatsura 楠木正行

kyō 卿

kyōgaku sasshin hyōgikai
教學刷新評議會

kyōiku ni kansuru chokugo
『教育ニ關スル勅語』

kyūjō jiken 宮城事件

Kyūshū teikoku daigaku
九州帝國大學

Maizuru 舞鶴

Maki Izumi no Kami (Maki Yasuomi)
眞木和泉守（眞木保臣）

Manshū jihen 滿洲事變

Manshū kenkoku daigaku / Manzhou jianguo daxue 滿洲建國大學

Maruyama Masao 丸山眞男

Matsudaira Mitsumichi 松平光通

Matsudaira Munenori 松平宗矩

Matsudaira Nagayoshi 松平永芳

Matsudaira Tadanao 松平忠直

Matsudaira Yoshinaga (Matsudaira Shungaku) 松平慶永（松平春嶽）

Matsudaira Yoshitami 松平慶民

Matsui Iwane 松井石根

Matsumoto Ayao 松本純郎

Meidōkan 明道館

Meiji 明治

Meiji ishin 明治維新

Mera 米良

Mera Noritada (Kikuchi Noritada)
米良則忠（菊池則忠）

Minakami 水上

Minamoto Sanetomo 源實朝

Minatogawa jinja 湊川神社

Minatogawa no tatakai 湊川の戰い

Minobe Tatsukichi 美濃部達吉

Minseitō 民政黨

Mito 水戸

Mitogaku 水戸學

monbushō 文部省

Monmu Tennō 文武天皇

Morishita Tatsunosuke 森下辰之助

Morito Tatsuo 森戸辰男

Motoori Norinaga 本居宣長

Murakami Tennō 村上天皇

Nagoya Tokimasa　名越時正

Nagumo Chūichi　南雲忠一

naidaijin　内大臣

naimushō　内務省

Nakamura Kichiji　中村吉治

Nakamura Kōya　中村孝也

nanbokuchō jidai　南北朝時代

Nanbokuchō seijunron　南北朝正閏論

nanchō　南朝

Nanjing Guomin Zhengfu
　南京國民政府

Nankō　楠公

Nankō musha gyōretsu　楠公武者行列

Nankōsai　楠公祭

nankō sūhai　楠公崇拝

Nanshiron　『楠子論』

Nawa Nagatoshi　名和長年

nenbutsu　念佛

Nichimanka kyōdō sengen
　日満華共同宣言

Nichiren　日蓮

Nichiren shugi　日蓮主義

Nihon　『日本』

Nihon chūkō　日本中興

Nihon dōgaku engenroku
　『日本道學淵源録』

Nihongaku kyōkai　日本學協會

Nihongaku sōsho　日本學叢書

Nihon kaizō hōan taikō
　『日本改造法案大綱』

Nihon seinenkan　日本青年館

Nihonshi no chūjiku　日本史の中軸

Nihon shisōshi kōza　日本思想史講座

Nihon shoki　『日本書紀』

Nikkō　日光

Ninigi no Mikoto　瓊瓊杵尊

niniroku jikeni　二・二六事件

Nippon seishin　日本精神

Nishida Mitsugi　西田税

Nishi Shin'ichirō　西晋一郎

Nitta Yoshisada　新田義貞

Nittō chikuonki　日東蓄音機

Nomonhan jiken　ノモンハン事件

Obata Toshirō　小畑敏四郎

Ōe no Masafusa　大江匡房

Ōhashi Totsuan　大橋訥庵

Okada Keisuke　岡田啓介

Oka Jirō　（Oka Hyōson）
　岡次郎　（岡彪邨）

Ōkawa Shūmei　大川周明

Ōnin no ran　應仁の亂

Onjōji　園城寺

Onozuka Kiheiji　小野塚喜平次

Ōtsu　大津

Pu Yi　溥儀

reikon no chikara 靈魂の力

rekishigaku kenkyūkai 歴史學研究會

Reiōzan Heisenji Engi
　『靈應山平泉寺録起』

ri 利

Rikken Seiyūkai 立憲政友會

rikkokushi 六國史

rikugun daigakkō 陸軍大學校

rikugun kenpei gakkō 陸軍憲兵學校

rikugun shikan gakkō 陸軍士官學校

rikugun Toyama gakko 陸軍戸山學校

risō 理想

Rokōkyō jiken 盧溝橋事件

Saigō Takamori　西郷隆盛

Saionji Kinmochi　西園寺公望

Saitō Makoto　齋藤實

Sakura Azumao　佐久良東雄

Sakurakai 櫻會

Sakuta Shōichi　作田莊一

sanbō honbu 参謀本部

sangatsu jiken 三月事件

sanreizan 三靈山

Satomi Kishio　里見岸雄

sei 聖

Seiseijuku 青々塾

seishi 正史

seishin 精神

seiyōshi gakka 西洋史學科

sengoku jidai 戰國時代

sensei 先生

sentetsu 先哲

Shiba Takatsune　斯波高経

Shibuya Inohiko　渋谷伊之彦

shichi hakushi 七博士

Shichiseisha 七生社

shigakkai 史學會

Shigaku zasshi 　『史學雜誌』

shikibu chōkan 式部長官

shikyoku 史局

Shimada Tōsuke　島田東助

Shimizu Mitsumi　清水光美

shin 眞

shinchoku 神勅

shindō jissen 臣道實踐

shinkoku 神國

shinmin 臣民

shinpan daimyō 親藩大名

Shinron 『新論』

shintaisei 新體制

Shinto wa saiten no kozoku
　「神道は祭天の古俗」

shiryō hensan gakari 資料編纂掛

shiryō hensanjo 史料編纂所

shishaku 子爵

shishi 志士

shogyō mujō 諸行無常

Shōhakujuku 松柏塾

Shōka sonjuku 松下村塾

Shōkonsha 招魂社

Shōwa　昭和

Shōwa ishin　昭和維新

Shōwa junnansha　昭和殉難者

shugo　守護

shuken　主權

Shukōkai　朱光會

Shushigaku　朱子學

shūshikan　修史館

shūshi no shō　「修史の詔」

sōhei　僧兵

Sondōkan　存道館

sonnō jōi　尊王攘夷

sōri daijin　聰理大臣

Sōtōshū　曹洞宗

Suika Shintō　垂加神道

sūmitsu'in　樞密院

Tachibana Akemi　橘曙覽

Taichō　泰澄

Tai'erzhuang　臺兒莊

taigi　大義

taigi meibun　大義名分

Taiheiki　『太平記』

Taika no kaishin　大化の改新

Taisei yokusankai　大政翼賛會

taisei yokusan no michi
　大政翼賛の道

Taishō　大正

taiten　大典

Taiyō　『太陽』

Takahashi Korekiyo　高橋是清

Takamatsu no miya Nobuhito
　高松宮宣仁

Takasugi Shinsaku　高杉晋作

Takayama Hikokurō　高山彦九郎

Tanaka Chigaku　田中智學

Tanaka Takashi　田中卓

Tanaka Yoshinari　田中義成

Tani Jinzan (Tani Shigetō)
　谷秦山（谷重遠）

Tateyama　立山

teikoku zaigō gunjinkai
　帝國在郷軍人會

Tendaishū　天台宗

tenjō mukyū no shinchoku
　天壤無窮の神勅

tenkō　轉向

Tenmu Tennō　天武天皇

tennō kikansetsu　天皇機關説

tennō kikansetsu ronsō
　天皇機關説論争

tennō shinsei　天皇親政

tennō shukensetsu　天皇主權説

Terada Takeshi　寺田剛

Terauchi Hisaichi　寺內壽一

Tōa shinchitsujo　東亞新秩序

tōchiken　統治權

tōchiken no shutai　統治權ノ主體

tōchiken wo sōranshi　統治權ヲ総覽シ

Tōhoku teikoku daigaku
　東北帝國大學

Tōjō Hideki　東條英機

Tokugawa Ieyasu　徳川家康

Tokugawa Mitsukuni　徳川光圀

Tokugawa Nariaki　徳川斉昭

Tokunaga Sakae　徳永榮

tokusetsu gunpō kaigi　特設軍法會議

Tokutomi Sohō　德富蘇峰

Tōkyō teikoku daigaku　東京帝國大學

Tomita Kenji　富田健治

tōseiha　統制派

Tōshōgū　東照宮

Tōyama Mitsuru　頭山満

Tsuji Masanobu　辻政信

Tsuji Zennosuke　辻善之助

Tsukuba　筑波

udai ittei　宇内一帝

Ueda Muneshige　上田宗重

Uesugi Shinkichi　上杉愼吉

Ugaki Kazushige　宇垣一成

Umeda Unpin　梅田雲浜

Ushijima Sadao　牛島貞雄

Wakabayashi Kyōsai　若林強齋

Wang Mang　王莽

Xie Fangde　謝枋得

Yamaga Sokō　山鹿素行

Yamagata Aritomo　山縣有朋

Yamagata Daini　山縣大弐

Yamamoto Isoroku　山本五十六

Yamazaki Ansai　山崎闇斎

Yasui Eiji　安井英二

Yasukuni jinja　靖國神社

yokusan　翼賛

Yonai Mitsumasa　米内光政

Yoshida Shōin　吉田松陰

Yoshida Tōko　吉田東篁

Yoshino　吉野

Yuasa Kurahei　湯淺倉平

Yūki Hideyasu (Matsudaira Hideyasu)
結城秀康　（松平秀康）

za　座

zaigai kenkyū　在外研究

zen　善

Zentsūji　善通寺

Zhang Jinghui　張景惠

Zhu Xi　朱熹

Bibliography

ABE Takeshi 1999, *Taiheiyō sensō to rekishigaku*. Tōkyō: Yoshikawa Kōbunkan.
阿部猛『太平洋戦争と歴史学』吉川弘文館。

ANDŌ Yūichirō 2021, *Echizen Fukui hanshu Matsudaira Shungaku—Meiji ishin wo mezashita Tokugawa ichimon*. Tōkyō: Heibonsha Shinsho.
安藤優一郎『越前福井藩主 松平春嶽—明治維新を目指した徳川一門』平凡社新書。

Asahi shinbunsha (ed.) 1942, *Sensen taishō kinkai*. Ōsaka: Asahi Shinbunsha.
朝日新聞社編『宣戦大詔謹解』朝日新聞社。

_______ *Yamasaki gunjin butai*, 20 May 1944. Tōkyō: Asahi Shinbunsha
朝日新聞社『山崎軍神部隊』朝日新聞社〈1944年5月20日〉。

AUER, James E. (ed.) 2006, *Who Was Responsible? From Marco Polo Bridge to Pearl Harbor*. Tōkyō: The Yomiuri Shinbun.

de BARY, Theodore / GLUCK, Carol / TIEDEMANN, Arthur E. (ed.) 2006, *Sources of Japanese Traditions, Part 2: 1868 to 2000* (Second Edition). New York: Columbia University Press.

BEARD, Charles 2003 (orig. published in 1948), *President Roosevelt and the Coming of the War, 1941: Appearances and Realities*. London: Routledge.

BENESCH, Oleg 2014, *Inventing the Way of the Samurai: Nationalism, Internationalism, and Bushido in Modern Japan*. Oxford: Oxford Univ. Press.

BERGER, Gordon M. 1977, *Parties Out of Power in Japan, 1931–1941*. Princeton: Princeton University Press.

BETSUMIYA Danrō 2012, *Shūsen kūdetā*. Tōkyō: Namiki Shobō.
　別宮暖朗『終戦クーデター』並木書房。

BIX, Herbert P. 2000, *Hirohito and the Making of Modern Japan*. New York:
　HarperCollins.

Bōeichō bōei kenkyūsho (ed.) 1968, *Hokutō hōmen rikugun sakusen 1—Attu no gyokusai
　(senshi sōsho 21)*. Tōkyō: Asagumo Shinbunsha.
　防衛庁防衛研修所編『北東方面陸軍作戦〈1〉—アッツの玉砕 (戦史叢書21)』
　朝雲新聞社。

BREEN, John (ed.) 2008, *Yasukuni, the War Dead, and the Struggle for Japan's Past*. New
　York: Columbia Univ. Press.

BROWNLEE, John 1997, *Japanese Historians and the National Myths, 1600-1945*.
　Vancouver: Univ. of British Columbia.

CHANG Chi-Yun 2012, *Confucianism: A Modern Interpretation*. Hangzhou: Zhejiang
　University Press.

COOK, Haruko T. & COOK, Theodore F. 1992, *Japan at War*. New York: The
　New Press.

CONRAD, Sebastian 1999, *Auf der Suche nach der verlorenen Nation: Geschichtsschreibung
　in Westdeutschland und Japan 1945-1960*. Göttingen: Vandenhoeck & Ruprecht.

Daidō gakuin (ed.) 1940, *Ronsō daini shū*. Shinkyō: Manshū Gyōsei Gakkai.
　大同學院編纂『論叢 第二輯』滿州行政學會。

DOWER, John W. 1987, *War Without Mercy: Race and Power in the Pacific War*.
　New York: Pantheon.

＿＿＿＿ 1999, *Embracing Defeat: Japan in the Wake of World War II*. New York: W.W.
　Norton & Co.

＿＿＿＿ 2012, *Ways of Forgetting, Way of Remembering: Japan in the Modern World*. New
　York: The New Press.

FRANK, Richard B. 1990, *Guadalcanal: The Definitive Account of the Landmark Battle*.
　New York: Random House.

＿＿＿＿ 1999, *Downfall—The End of the Imperial Japanese Empire*. New York: Penguin.

________ 2020, *Tower of Skulls: A History of the Asia-Pacific War: July 1937-May 1942*. New York: W. W. Norton & Co.

FRIDAY, Karl F. (ed.) 2012, *Japan Emerging: Premodern History to 1850*. Boulder: Westview Press.

FURUKAWA Takahisa 2005, *Shōwa senchūki no gikai to gyōsei*. Tōkyō: Yoshikawa Kōbunkan.
古川隆久『昭和戦中期の議会と行政』吉川弘文館。

GOBLE, Andrew 1996, *Kenmu: Go-Daigos Revolution*. Harvard: Harvard East Asian Monographs.

GRIFFIS, William E. 1876, *The Mikado's Empire: Book I, History of Japan, from 660 B.C. to 1872 A.D.; Book II, Personal Experiences, Observations, and Studies in Japan, 1870-1874*. New York: Harper & Brothers.

HALL, Robert King (ed.) / GAUNTLETT, John Owen 1949, *Kokutai no Hongi— Cardinal Principles of the National Entity of Japan*. Cambridge (Mass.): Harvard University Press.

HANDŌ Kazutoshi 1997, *Senshi no isho*. Tōkyō: Bunshun Bunko.
半藤一利『戦士の遺書』文春文庫。

________ 2006, *Ketteiban—Nihon no ichiban nagai hi*. Tōkyō: Bunshun Bunko.
半藤一利『決定版 日本のいちばん長い日』文春文庫。

HANDŌ Kazutoshi & YUKAWA Yutaka 2015, *Genbaku no ochita hi— "ketteiban"*. Tōkyō: PHP Bunko.
半藤一利・湯川豊『原爆の落ちた日 "決定版"』PHP文庫。

HARADA Kumao 1951, *Saionji Kinmochi to seikyoku 5*. Iwanami Shoten.
原田熊雄『西園寺公と政局　第五巻』岩波書店。

HARDACRE, Helen 2017, *Shinto: A History*. New York: Oxford Univ. Press.

HASEGAWA Tsuyoshi 2006, *Racing the Enemy: Stalin, Truman and the Surrender of Japan*. Harvard: Belknap Press.

HATA Ikuhiko 1984, *Hirohito tennō itsutsu no ketsudan*. Tōkyō: Kōdansha.
秦郁彦『裕仁天皇五つの決断』講談社。

HAYATA Yoshihiko / SHIRASAKI Shōichirō / MATSUURA Yoshinori / KIMURA
Ryō 2014, *Fukuiken no rekishi (kenshi 18)*. Tōkyō: Yamakawa Shuppansha.
隼田嘉彦・白崎昭一郎・松浦義則・木村亮『福井県の歴史 (県史18)』山川出版社。

HIRAIZUMI Kiyoshi 1926, *Chūsei ni okeru seishin seikatsu*. Tōkyō: Shibundō.
平泉澄『中世に於ける精神生活』至文堂。

———— 1926, *Waga rekishikan*. Tōkyō: Shibundō.
平泉澄『我が歴史觀』至文堂。

———— 1926, *Chūsei ni okeru shaji to shakai to no kankei*. Tōkyō: Shibundō.
平泉澄『中世に於ける社寺と社會との関係』至文堂。

———— (ed.) 1927, *Tōshōgūshi*. Nikkō: Tōshōgū Shamusho.
平泉澄編『東照宮史』東照宮社務所。

———— 1928, *Nihon jidō bunko 2—Nihon rekishi monogatari (chū)*. Tōkyō: Arusu.
平泉澄『日本兒童文庫—日本歴史物語 (中) 』アルス。

———— (ed.) 1929, *Gōto Tokudō gengan monshū*. Tōkyō: Shibundō.
平泉澄校『江都督納言願文集』至文堂。

———— (ed.) 1932, *Ansai sensei to Nihon seishin*. Tōkyō: Shibundō.
平泉澄編『闇斎先生と日本精神』至文堂。

———— 1932, *Kokushigaku no kotsuzui*. Tōkyō: Shibundō.
平泉澄『國史學の骨髄』至文堂。

———— 1933, *Bushidō no fukkatsu*. Tōkyō: Shibundō.
平泉澄『武士道の復活』至文堂。

———— (ed.) 1933, *Jinnō shōtōki 1-4*. Tōkyō: Sanshūsha.
平泉澄編纂『神皇正統記 4冊』三秀舎。

———— 1934, *Shisō mondai shōgō 6—Kakumeiron*. Tōkyō: Monbushō.
平泉澄『思想問題小輯 6—革命論』文部省。

———— 1934, *Chū to gi*. Kanazawa: Ishikawaken Keisatsubu.
平泉澄『忠と義』石川縣警察部。

———— 1934, *Kenmu chūkō no hongi*. Tōkyō: Shibundō.
平泉澄『建武中興の本義』至文堂。

———— 1936, *Kokushi kōwa*. Tōkyō: Rikugun Daigakkō.
平泉澄『國史講話』陸軍大學校。

———— 1936, *Banbutsu ruten*. Tōkyō: Shibundō.
平泉澄『萬物流轉』至文堂。

————, ›Hijōji ni odoru Yamato damashii‹, in *Kagoshima Shinbun*, 12-23 July 1938.
平泉澄「非常時に踊る大和魂」〈『鹿兒島新聞』昭和13年7月12日～23日〉。

———— 1939, *Hakkō ichiu*. Tōkyō: Teikoku Zaigō Gunjinkai Honbu.
平泉澄『八紘一宇』帝國在郷軍人會本部。

———— 1939, *Kokutai shikan ni motozuku Nihon gaikōshi*. Tōkyō: Gaimushō.
平泉澄『國體史觀に基づく日本外交史』外務省。

———— 1940, *Dentō*. Tōkyō: Shibundō.
平泉澄『傳統』至文堂。

———— 1940, *Kenmu no chūkō ni tsuite*. Tōkyō: Gaimushō.
平泉澄『建武中興について』外務省。

———— 1941, *Kigen nisen roppyakunen wo mukaete*. Nagoya: Nagoyashi Shakaikyō.
平泉澄『紀元二千六百年を迎へて』名古屋市社會教。

———— 1941, *Kikuchi kinnōshi*. Tōkyō: Kikuchishi Kinnō Kenshōkai.
平泉澄『菊池勤王史』菊池氏勤王顯彰會。

————, ›Tenpei ni teki nashi‹, in *Shūkan Asahi*, 17 January 1942.
平泉澄「天兵に敵なし」〈『週刊朝日』昭和17年1月17日〉。

————, ›Kokushi wo tsuranuku mono‹, in *Gendai* 23-1, January 1942.
平泉澄「國史をつらぬくもの」〈『現代23:1』〉。

————, ›Yūkyū nisen roppyaku ninen‹, in *Shūkan Asahi*, 15 February 1942.
平泉澄「悠久二千六百二年」〈『週刊朝日』昭和17年2月15日〉。

————, ›Nankō nanasei no nengan‹, in *Asahi Shinbun*, 9 March 1942.
平泉澄「楠公七生の念願」〈『朝日新聞』昭和17年3月9日〉。

————, ›Hana no gotoku‹, in *Asahi Shinbun*, 15 March 1942.
平泉澄「花の如く」〈『朝日新聞』昭和17年3月15日〉。

————, ›Tenka no odaiji‹, in *Gendai* 24-1, April 1942.
平泉澄「天下の御大事」〈『現代24:1』〉。

———— 1942, *Hiraizumi Kiyoshi Hakase kōwa – kōkoku goji no michi*. Etajima: Kaigun Heigakkō.
平泉澄『平泉澄博士講話―皇國護持の道』海軍兵學校。

———— 1943, *Kaitei—Kokushi gaisetsu*. Tōkyō: Keimeisha.
平泉澄『改訂 國史概説』啓明社。

———— 1943, *Tenpei ni teki nashi*. Tōkyō: Shibundō.
平泉澄『天兵に敵なし』至文堂。

________ 1943, *Chūshi no gaku*. Fukui: Fukui Kyōikukai.
平泉澄『忠死の學』福井教育會。

________, ›*Ichinichi no hōkō jūnen no koku'un*‹, in *Shūkan Asahi*, 5 December 1943.
平泉澄「一日の奉公十年の國運」〈『週刊朝日』昭和18年12月5日〉。

________, ›*Gōsō no kishō wo kenji shite*‹, in *Tōkyō Shinbun*, 27 December 1944.
平泉澄「剛操の気象を堅持して」〈『東京新聞』昭和19年12月27日〉。

________, ›*Haru ni akete*‹ (part 1 & 2), in *Mainichi Shinbun*, 1-2 January 1945.
平泉澄「春にあけて　上・下」〈『毎日新聞』昭和20年1月1日〜2日〉。

________, ›*Warera no sosen wa kaku tatakatta — Takefusa ni tsuzuke — genkō wa motto kurushikatta*‹, in *Mainichi Shinbun*, 7 June 1945.
平泉澄「我らの祖先はかく戦った　武房に続け　元寇はもっと苦しかった」
〈『毎日新聞』昭和20年6月7日〉。

________ 1952, *Bashō no omokage*. Tōkyō: Nihon Shoin.
平泉澄『芭蕉の俤』日本書院。

________ (ed.) 1953, *Izumo no kuni fudoki no kenkyū*. Izumo: Izumo Taisha Gosengū Hōsankai.
平泉澄監修『出雲国風土記の研究』出雲大社御遷宮奉賛会。

________ 1953, *Taichō washō denki*. Katsuyama: Hakusan Jinja.
平泉澄校訂『泰澄和尚伝記』白山神社。

________ 1954, *Nawa seika*. Tōkyō: Nihon Bunka Kenkyūsho.
平泉澄『名和世家』日本文化研究所。

________ (ed.) 1954, *Kitabatake Chikafusa kō no kenkyū*. Tōkyō: Nihongaku Kenkyūsho.
平泉澄監修『北畠親房公の研究』日本学研究所。

________ (ed.) 1957, *Dainihonshi no kenkyū*. Tōkyō: Tachibana Shobō.
平泉澄編『大日本史の研究』立花書房。

________ 1963, *Kaisetsu Kinsei Nihon kokuminshi*. Tōkyō: Jiji Tsūshinsha.
平泉澄『解説近世日本国民史』時事通信社。

________ 1963-1967, *Fuso no sokuseki* (vol. 1-5). Tōkyō: Jiji Tsūshinsha.
平泉澄『父祖の足跡（正・続・続々・再続・三続）』時事通信社。

________ 1964, *Kanrin shihitsu*. Tōkyō: Tachibana Shobō.
平泉澄『寒林史筆』立花書房。

________ 1964, *Kakumei to dentō*. Tōkyō: Jiji Tsūshinsha.
平泉澄『革命と傳統』時事通信社。

________ (ed.) 1968-1971, *Rekishi zanka* (vol. 1-5). Tōkyō: Jiji Tsūshinsha.
平泉澄監修『歴史残花（全五巻）』時事通信社。

________ 1970, *Kaisetsu Kajin no kigū*. Tōkyō: Jiji Tsūshinsha.
平泉澄『解説佳人之奇遇』時事通信社。

________ 1970, *Meiji no genryū*. Tōkyō: Jiji Tsūshinsha.
平泉澄『明治の源流』時事通信社。

________ 1970, *Shōnen Nihonshi*. Tōkyō: Jiji Tsūshinsha.
平泉澄『少年日本史』時事通信社。

________ 1972, *Sentetsu wo aogu*. Tōkyō: Nihongaku Kyōkai.
平泉澄『先哲を仰ぐ』（増補版）日本學協会。

________ 1973, *Nankō – sono chūretsu to yokō*. Kagoshima: Kagoshima Shuppankai.
平泉澄『楠公—その忠烈と余香』鹿島出版会。

________ (ed.) 1975, *Bonanki*. Gifu: Gifuken Kyōiku Konwakai.
平泉澄編『慕楠記』岐阜県教育懇話会。

________ 1975, *Yamabiko*. Tōkyō: Tachibana Shobō.
平泉澄『山彦』立花書房。

________ 1977, *Nihon no higeki to risō*. Tōkyō: Hara Shobō.
平泉澄『日本の悲劇と理想』原書房。

________ 1979, *Monogatari Nihonshi* (vol. 1-3). Tōkyō: Kōdansha Gakujutsu Bunko.
平泉澄『物語日本史　上・中・下』講談社学術文庫。

________ 1980, *Meiji no kōki*. Tōkyō: Nihongaku Kyōkai.
平泉澄『明治の光輝』日本學協会。

________ 1980, *Higeki jūsō*. Ise: Kōgakkan Daigaku Shuppanbu.
平泉澄『悲劇縦走』皇學館大學出版部。

________ 1986, *Shukyū no hito—Daisaigō*. Tōkyō: Hara Shobō.
平泉澄『首丘の人—大西郷』原書房。

________ 1995, *Kono michi wo yuku—Kanrinshi kaikoroku.* (Unpublished.)
平泉澄『この道を行く—寒林子回顧録』私家版。

________ 1997-2002, *The Story of Japan* (vol. 1-3). Ise: Seisei Kikaku.

________ 1998, *Sentetsu wo aogu* (Third revised edition). Tōkyō: Kinseisha.
平泉澄『先哲を仰ぐ・三訂版』錦正社。

________ 2005, *Sanga ari (zen)*. Tōkyō: Kinseisha.
平泉澄『山河あり（全）』錦正社。

_______ 2014, *Hiraizumi Kiyoshi hakase shintō ronshō*. Tōkyō: Kinseisha.
平泉澄『平泉澄博士神道論抄』錦正社。

_______ 2016, *Zoku Hiraizumi Kiyoshi hakase shintō ronshō*. Tōkyō: Kinseisha.
平泉澄『続・平泉澄博士神道論抄』錦正社。

HIRAIZUMI Kiyoshi & KOBAYASHI Kenzō (ed.) 1934, *Jinnō shōtōki*. Ishikawa:
Shirayama Hime Jinja.
平泉澄解説・小林健三校訂『神皇正統記』白山比咩神社。

HIRAIZUMI Kiyoshi & TERADA Takeshi (ed.) 1938-1943, *Ōhashi Totsuan sensei zenshū*
(vol. 1-3). Tōkyō: Shibundō.
平泉澄・寺田剛編『大橋訥庵先生全集　上・中・下』至文堂。

HIRAIZUMI Wataru, ›*Chichi Hiraizumi Kiyoshi no tsukue ni okareta shashin*‹, in *Bungei
Shunjū*, August 2005.
平泉渉「父・平泉澄の机に置かれた写真」〈『文藝春秋』2005年8月〉。

HIRATA Toshiharu 1967, *Nihon no kenkoku to nigatsu jūichinichi*. Tōkyō: Kōyō Shobō.
平田俊春『日本の建国と二月十一日』甲陽書房。

_______ 1967, *Nihon shoki to kenkoku kinen no hi*. Tōkyō: Arupususha.
平田俊春『日本書紀と建国記念日』アルプス社。

HIROSE Shigemi, ›*Hiraizumi Kiyoshi sensei to Ōkawa Shūmei hakase*‹, in *Nihon*, October-
November 2007.
廣瀬重見「平泉澄先生と大川周明博士」〈『日本』2007年10月號～11月號〉。

HORI Yukio 1997, *Senzen no kokkashugi undōshi*. Tōkyō: Sanrei Shobō.
堀幸雄『戦前の国家主義運動史』三嶺書房。

HORNFISCHER, James D. 2012, *Neptune's Inferno: The U.S. Navy at Guadalcanal*. New
York: Bantam Books.

HOSAKA Masayasu 2007, *Shōwashi no taiga wo yuku "Yasukuni" to iu nayami*. Tōkyō:
Mainichi Shinbunsha.
保阪正康『昭和史の大河を往く「靖国」という悩み』毎日新聞社。

INOUE Tetsujirō / UEDA Kazutoshi (ed.) / HIRAIZUMI Kiyoshi (commentary) 1934,
Nihon shoki — Dainihon bunko kokushihen. Tōkyō: Shunyōdō.
井上哲次郎・上田萬年監修・平泉澄校訂『日本書記　大日本文庫　国史篇』春陽堂。

ITŌ Hirobumi (transl. by ITŌ Mijoji) 1889, *Commentaries on the Constitution of the Empire of Japan*. Tōkyō: IGIRISU-HŌRITSU GAKKO.

ITŌ Takashi (orig. 1978), ›*Tōkyō daigakushi kyūshokuin intabyū 3 — Hiraizumi Kiyoshi shi intabyū 1-6*‹, in *Tōkyō daigakushi kiyō 13-18*, March 1995 - March 2000.
伊藤隆編「東京大学旧職員インタビュー(3)　平泉澄氏インタビュー」
『東京大学史紀要』第13号〜第18号、1995年3月〜2000年3月。

IWATA Masataka, ›*Misui ni owatta kirikomi keikaku (ni niroku jiken no shinjijitsu)*‹, in *Chūō kōron*, March 1992, 320-329.
岩田正孝「未遂に終わった斬り込み計画 (2.26事件の新事実)」〈『中央公論』
1992年3月号〉。

JANSEN, Marius 2000, *The Making of Modern Japan*. Cambridge (Mass.): Harvard University Press.

KAMEI-DYCHE, Rieko 2016, ›An Engagement with the Scholarship on Mitogaku, from the 1930s to the Present‹. Tōkyō: Hitotsubashi University — Daigaku Kyōiku Kenkyū Kaihatsu Sentā, *Jinbun shizen kenkyū 10* (一橋大学大学教育研究開発センタ ー　人文・自然研究 第 10 号), 74-146.

KANOKOGI Kazunobu (ed.) 1941, *Kōkokugaku taikō*. Tōkyō: Dōbun Shoin.
鹿子木員信編『皇國學大綱』同文書院。

Katsuyamashi (ed.) 2017, *Hakusan Heisenji — yomigaeru shūkyō toshi*. Tōkyō: Yoshikawa Kōbunkan.
勝山市編『白山平泉寺—よみがえる宗教都市』吉川弘文館。

KAWAMURA Noriko 2015, *Emperor Hirohito and the Pacific War*. Seattle and London: University of Washington Press.

Keisatsu kōshūsho hensan 1943, *Keisatsu kōwaroku*. Tōkyō: Shōkadō Shoten.
警察講習所編纂『警察講話録』松華堂書店。

Kenmugikai (ed.) 1939, *Godaigo tennō hōsan ronbunshū*. Tōkyō: Shibundō.
建武義會編『後醍醐天皇奉賛論文集』至文堂。

Kenmu no chūkō roppyakunen kinenkai (ed.) 1934, *Kenmu no chūkō*. Tōkyō: Kenmu no chūkō roppyakunen kinenkai.
建武中興六百年記念會編『建武中興』建武中興六百年記念會。

________ (ed.) 1934, *Kenmu no chūkō roppyakunen kinenkai jigyō hōkoku*. Tōkyō: Kenmu no chūkō roppyakunen kinenkai.
建武中興六百年記念會編『建武中興六百年記念會事業報告』建武中興六百年記念會。

KISHIMOTO Mio / KATŌ Tomoyasu / KAWAKITA Minoru *et al.* (ed.) 1997, *Rekishigaku jiten 5 — rekishika to sono sakuhin*. Tōkyō: Kōbunkan.
岸本美緒・加藤友康・川北稔ほか(編集)『歴史学事典【第5巻　歴史家とその作品】』弘文堂。

KOBAYASHI Kinzō 2002, *Hakutō—Manshūkoku kenkoku daigaku*. Tōkyō: Shinjinbutsu Ōraisha.
小林金三『白塔 満洲国建国大学』新人物往来社。

Kōfūkan henshūsho 1935, *Chūgaku kokubun kyōkasho kyōju bikō maki 5*. Tōkyō: Kōfūkan Shoten.
光風館編輯所『中學國文教科書教授備考　巻五』光風館書店。

KONADA Toshiharu & KATAOKA Noriaki 2006, *Tokkō kaiten sen—Kaiten tōkkōtai taichō no kaisō*. Tōkyō: Kōjinsha.
小灘利春・片岡紀明『特攻回天戦—回天特攻隊隊長の回想』光人社。

KONOE Fumimaro 1940, *Senjika no kokumin ni okeru Konoe shushō ensetsushū*. Tōkyō: Tōkōsha.
近衛文麿『戰時下の國民におくる近衛首相演説集』東晃社。

KOSCHMANN, Victor J. 1987, *The Mito Ideology: Discourse, Reform, and Insurrection in Late Tokugawa Japan, 1790-1864*. Berkeley: University of California Press.

KOYAMA Tsunemi 1989, *Tennō kikansetsu to kokumin kyōiku*. Tōkyō: Akademia Shuppankai.
小山常美『天皇機関説と国民教育』アカデミア出版会。

KREBS, Gerhard 2010, *Japan im Pazifischen Krieg—Herrschaftssystem, politische Willensbildung und Friedenssuche*. München: Iudicium.

________ 2021, *Spannungen im japanischen Kaiserhaus*. München: Iudicium.

KUDŌ Miyoko 2006, *Ware Sugamo ni shutto sezu*. Tōkyō: Nihon Keizai Shinbunsha.
工藤美代子『われ巣鴨に出頭せず』日本経済新聞社。

LEE, Edwin B., ›Nichiren and Nationalism: The Religious Patriotism of Tanaka Chigaku‹, in *Monumenta Nipponica* 30/1, Spring 1975, 19-35.

Mainichi shinbun "Yasukuni" shuzaihan (ed.) 2007, *Yasukuni sengo hishi—A-kyūsenpan wo gōshi shita otoko*. Tōkyō: Mainichi Shinbunsha.
毎日新聞「靖国」取材班『靖国戦後秘史—A級戦犯を合祀した男』毎日新聞社。

MAIR, Michael & WALDRON, Joy 2014, *Kaiten—Japan's Secret Manned Suicide Submarine and the First American Ship it Sank in WWII*. New York: Berkley Books.

MARUOKA Hideo (ed.) 1935, *Bushidō kyōhon*. Uwajima: Kōbunsha.
丸岡秀夫編『武士道教本』廣文社。

MARUYAMA Masao 1974, *Studies in the Intellectual History of Tokugawa Japan*. Tōkyō and Princeton: Tōkyō Univ. Press & Princeton Univ. Press.

———— 1997, *Loyalität und Rebellion*. München: Iudicium.

———— 2006, *Maruyama Masao kaikoroku* (vol. 1 & 2). Tōkyō: Iwanami Shoten.
丸山眞男『丸山眞男回顧録　上・下』岩波書店。

MATSUSHIMA Eiichi (ed.) 1952, *Nihon rekishi kōza 1 rekishi rironhen*. Tōkyō: Kawade Shobō.
松島榮一編『日本歴史講座　第1巻　歴史理論篇』河出書房。

McCULLOUGH, Helen Craig 2008, *The Taiheiki—A Chronicle of Medieval Japan*. Tōkyō: Tuttle Publishing.

McVEIGH, Brian J. 2003, *Nationalisms of Japan: Managing and Mystifying Identity*. Lanham (Maryland): Rowman & Littlefield Publishers.

MEINECKE, Friedrich, ›Kausalitäten und Werte in der Geschichte‹, in *Historische Zeitschrift* 137, H.-1 1928, 1-27.

———— 1965, *Zur Theorie und Philosophie der Geschichte, Werke Bd. IV*. München / Berlin: Oldenbourg.

MEHL, Margaret, ›Scholarship and Ideology in Conflict: The Kume Affair, 1892‹, in *Monumenta Nipponica* 48/3 1993, 337-357.

————, ›German Influence on Historical Scholarship in Meiji Japan‹, in Historiographical Institute at the University of Tokyo 2002, *The Past, Present and Future of History and Historical Sources—A Symposium to Commemorate 100 years of Publications of the Historiographical Institute*, 225-246.

_________ 2017, *History and the State in Nineteenth-Century Japan: The World, the Nation and the Search for a Modern Past* (Second Edition): Copenhagen: The Sound Book Press.

MITTER, Rana 2013, *China's War with Japan, 1937-1945*. London: Allan Lane.

MIURA Hideyuki 2017, *Goshiki no niji—Manshū kenkoku daigaku sotsugyōseitachi no sengo*. Tōkyō: Shūeisha Bunko.
三浦英之『五色の虹 満州建国大学卒業生たちの戦後』集英社文庫。

MIYAMOTO Masafumi 2011, *Umi no tokkō "kaiten"*. Tōkyō: Kadogawa Sofia Bunko.
宮本雅史『海の特攻「回天」』角川ソフィア文庫。

MORRIS, Ivan I. 1988 (orig. 1975), *The Nobility of Failure: Tragic Heroes in the History of Japan*. New York: Farrar Straus & Giroux.

NAGOYA Tokimasa 1986, *Shinpan—Mito Mitsukuni*. Tōkyō: Kinseisha.
名越時正『新版・水戸光圀』錦正社。

Naimushō keihokyoku (ed.) 1939, *Keisatsu kanbu Yokuonkan kōwaroku*. Tōkyō: Keisatsu Kyōkai.
内務省警保局編『警察幹部浴恩館講話録』警察協會。

NAKAMURA Masanori 1992, *The Japanese Monarchy: Ambassador Joseph Grew and the Making of the 'Symbol Emperor System,' 1931-1991*. New York: M.E. Sharpe.

NAKAMURA Takafusa 1998, *A History of Shōwa Japan, 1926-1989*. Tōkyō: University of Tōkyō Press.

NEUMANN, Florian 2011, *Politisches Denken im Japan des frühen 20. Jahrhunderts: Das Beispiel Uesugi Shinkichi (1878-1929)*. München: Iudicium.

_________, ›Die „*kokutai*-Wissenschaft" von Satomi Kishio (1897-1974)‹, in *OAG Notizen*, 02/2014, 25-50.

_________, ›Ōkawa Shūmei und der Weg zur „Shōwa-Erneuerung"‹, in *OAG Notizen*, 02/2015, 11-39.

_________, ›Ōkawa Shūmei und Japans Krieg in Ostasien‹, in *OAG Notizen*, 11/2015, 11-50.

_________, ›Hiraizumi Kiyoshi und der „Geist" der japanischen Geschichte‹, in *OAG Notizen*, 03/2017, 10-39.

________, ›Hiraizumi Kiyoshi – Die Kriegsjahre‹, in *OAG Notizen*, 04/2018, 10-46.

________, ›Hiraizumi Kiyoshi – Die Nachkriegszeit‹, in *OAG Notizen*, 09/2019, 21-58.

Nihon bunka kenkyūkai (ed.) 1958, *Jinmu tennō kigenron: kigensetsu no tadashii mikata*. Tōkyō: Tachibana Shobō.
日本文化研究会編『神武天皇紀元論: 紀元節の正しい見方』立花書房。

Nihon bunka kyōkai (ed.) 1937, *Kyōgaku sasshin hyōgikai tōshin oyobi kengi*. Tōkyō: Nihon Bunka Kyōkai.
日本文化協會編『教學刷新評議會答申及ビ建議』日本文化協會。

Nihon koten gakkai (ed.) 1936, *Yamazaki Ansai zenshū* (vol. 1-2). Tōkyō: Nihon koten gakkai.
日本古典學會編『山崎闇斎全集 2冊』日本古典學會。

________ (ed.) 1937, *Zoku Yamazaki Ansai zenshū* (vol. 1-3) Tōkyō: Nihon koten gakkai.
日本古典學會編『續山崎闇斎全集 3冊』日本古典學會。

NISHI Junzō, ABE Ryūichi, MARUYAMA Masao (ed.) 1980, *Nihon shisō taikei 31: Yamazaki Ansai gakuha*. Tōkyō: Iwanami Shoten.
西順蔵・阿部隆一・丸山眞男校注『日本思想大系〈31〉山崎闇斎学派』岩波書店。

Ōkawa Shūmei kankei monjo kankōkai (ed.) 1998, *Ōkawa Shūmei kankei monjo*. Tōkyō: Fuyō Shobō Shuppan.
大川周明関係文書刊行会編『大川周明関係文書』芙蓉書房出版。

Ōkawa Shūmei kenshōkai (ed.) 1986, *Ōkawa Shūmei nikki*. Tōkyō: Iwazaki Gakujutsu Shuppansha.
大川周明顕彰会『大川周明日記』岩崎学術出版社。

OOMS, Herman 1989, *Tokugawa Ideology: Early Constructs 1570-1680*. Princeton: Princeton Univ. Press.

Ōsakafu keisatsubu keimuka 1937, *Nippon seishin dainihen*. Ōsaka: Matsumotogō Insatsusho.
大阪府警察部警務課『日本精神　第二篇』松本號印刷所。

ŌTAKA Masajirō 1959, *Dainiji taisen sekininron*. Tōkyō: Jiji Tsūshinsha.
大鷹正次郎『第二次大戦責任論』時事通信社。

PIKE, Francis 2015, *Hirohito's War: The Pacific War, 1941-1945*. London, New York: Bloomsbury Publishing.

RUOFF, Kenneth 2010, *Imperial Japan at its Zenith: The Wartime Celebration of the Empire's 2,600th Anniversary*. Ithaca, London: Cornell Univ. Press.

SATŌ Nobuo, ›*Kōkoku shikan*‹, in *Rekishigaku kenkyū* 309, February 1966.
佐藤伸雄「皇国史観」〈『歴史学研究』第309号、1966年2月〉。

SCHMIDT, Donald 2005, *The Folly of War: American Foreign Policy, 1898-2005*. New York: Algora Publishing

SEIKE Motoyoshi 1995, *Senzen Shōwa nashonarizumu no shomondai*. Tōkyō: Kinseisha.
清家基良『戦前昭和ナショナリズムの諸問題』錦正社。

SHILLONY, Ben-Ami 1973, *Revolt in Japan: The Young Officers and the February 26, 1936 Incident*. Princeton: Princ eton Univ. Press.

Shinchōsha (ed.) 1933, *Nippon seishin kōza dai 1 kan*. Tōkyō: Shinchōsha.
新潮社編『日本精神講座 第一巻』新潮社。

SHISHIDA Fumiaki, ›*Kenkoku daigaku no kyōiku to Ishiwara Kanji*‹, in *Waseda daigaku ningen kagaku kenkyū* 6-1, 1993, 109-123.
志々田文明「建国大学の教育と石原莞爾」〈『早稲田大学人間科学研究 第6巻 第1号』1993年。〉

_______ 2003, *Manshūkoku Kenkoku daigaku ni okeru budō kyōiku. Doctor thesis at Waseda University*.
志々田文明『満洲国・建国大学に於ける武道教育』早稲田大学人間科学博士学位論文。

SHŌGUCHI Yasuhiro 2012, *Kisukatō kiseki no tettai—Kimura Masatomi chūshō no shōgai*. Tōkyō: Shinchō Bunko.
将口泰浩『キスカ島 奇跡の撤退—木村昌福中将の生涯』新潮文庫。

_______ 2017, *Gokuhi shirei—kōtō goji sakusen*. Tōkyō: Tokuma Shoten.
将口泰浩『極秘司令 皇統護持作戦』徳間書店。

STINNETT, Robert B. 2000, *Day of Deceit: The Truth about FDR and Pearl Harbor*. New York: The Free Press.

SYMONDS, Craig L. 2011, *The Battle of Midway*. New York: Oxford Univ. Press.

TACHIBANA Takashi 2005, *Tennō to Tōdai* (vol. 1 & 2). Tōkyō: Bungei Shunjū.
立花隆『天皇と東大　上・下』文芸春秋刊。

TAKANO Kunio 1989, *Tennōsei kokka no kyōikuron—kyōgaku sasshin hyōgikai no kenkyū*. Tōkyō: Azumino Shobō.
高野邦夫『天皇制国家の教育論—教学刷新評議会の研究』あずみの書房。

TAKESHITA Masahiko, ›*Anami rikushō no shūsenji no shinji*‹, in *Gunji shigaku*, August 1967, 87-104.
竹下正彦「平泉史学と陸軍(回想)」〈『軍事史学』1967年8月〉。

———, ›*Hiraizumi shigaku to rikugun*‹, in *Gunji shigaku*, May 1969, 110-115.
竹下正彦「平泉史学と陸軍(回想)」〈『軍事史学』1966年5月〉。

TANAKA Nobumasa 2002, *Yasukuni no sengoshi*. Tōkyō: Iwanami Shinsho.
田中伸尚『靖国の戦後史』岩波新書。

TANAKA Takashi 2000, *Hiraizumi shigaku to kōkoku shikan*. Ise: Seisei Kikaku.
田中卓『平泉史学と皇国史観』青々企画。

——— 2012, *Hiraizumi shigaku no shinzui*. Tōkyō: Kokusho Kankōkai.
田中卓『平泉史学の神髄』国書刊行会.

——— (ed.) 1998, *Hiraizumi hakase shironshō*. Ise: Seisei Kikaku.
田中卓編『平泉博士史論抄』青々企画。

——— (ed.) 2004, *Hiraizumi Kiyoshi hakase zenchosaku shōkai*. Tōkyō: Bensei Shuppan.
田中卓編『平泉澄博士全著作紹介』勉誠出版。

TANKHA, Brij 2006, *Kita Ikki and the Making of Modern Japan*. Honolulu: University of Hawaii Press.

TANSILL, Charles 1952, *Back Door to War: The Roosevelt Foreign Policy, 1933-1941*. Washington DC: Regnery.

TATAMIYA Eitarō 2000, *Kami no kuni to chōrekishika Hiraizumi Kiyoshi*. Tōkyō: Yūzankaku.
田々宮英太郎『神の国と超歴史家 平泉澄』雄山閣。

The Foreign Affairs Association of Japan 1938, *Politics and Political Parties in Japan*. Tōkyō: Kenkyūsha Press.

Tōdai jūhachi shikai (ed.) 1968, *Gakuto shutsujin no kiroku.* Tōkyō: Chūkō Shinsho.
東大十八史会編『学徒出陣の記録』中公新書。

TODAKA Kazushige 2018, *Tokkō—Shirarezaru uchimaku.* Tōkyō: PHP Shinsho.
戸高一成『特攻 知られざる内幕』PHP新書。

TOLAND, John 2001, *The Rising Sun: The Decline and Fall of the Japanese Empire 1936-1945.* London: Penguin.

TOLLEY, Kemp, ›The Strange Assignment of USS Lanikai‹, in *U.S. Naval Institute Proceedings* 88-9, September 1962, 70-83.

_______ 1973, *Cruise of the Lanikai: Incitement to War.* Annapolis: Naval Institute Press.

TSUNODA Fusako 2015 (1980), *Isshi, daizai wo shasu—rikugun daijin Anami Korechika.* Tōkyō: Chikuma Bunko.
角田房子『一死、大罪を謝す 陸軍大臣阿南惟幾』ちくま文庫。

UEDA Kiyoshi 2008, *Hiraizumi Kiyoshi (1895-1984): 'Spiritual history' in the Service of the Nation in Twentieth Century Japan.* Ann Arbor: University of Toronto.

UEMURA Kazuhide 2004, *Maruyama Masao to Hiraizumi Kiyoshi.* Tōkyō: Kashiwa Shobō.
植村和秀『丸山眞男と平泉澄』柏書房。

_______ 2010, *Shōwa no shisō.* Tōkyō: Kōdansha.
植村和秀『昭和の思想』講談社。

UESUGI Shinkichi (ed.) 1913, *Hozumi Yatsuka hakushi ronbunshū.* Tōkyō: Yūhikaku.
上杉愼吉編『穂積八束博士論文集』有斐閣。

UTLEY, Jonathan G. 2005 (orig. published in 1985), *Going to War with Japan, 1937-1941.* New York: Fordham Univ. Press.

VARLEY, Paul H. 1971, *Imperial Restoration in Medieval Japan.* New York: Columbia University Press.

_______ (tr.) 1980, *A Chronicle of Gods and Sovereigns: Jinnō Shōtōki of Kitabatake Chikafusa.* New York: Columbia Univ. Press.

WAKABAYASHI, Bob Tadashi (ed.) 1998, *Modern Japanese Thought.* Cambridge (Mass.): Harvard Univ. Press.

WAKAI Toshiaki 2006, *Hiraizumi Kiyoshi—Mikuni no tame ni ware tsukusanamu.* Tōkyō: Mineruva Shobō.
若井敏明『平泉澄—み国のために我つくさなむ』ミネルヴァ書房。

WATANABE Yōji 2000, *Itan no sora—Taiheiyō sensō Nihon gunyōki hiroku.* Tōkyō: Bunshun Bunko.
渡辺洋二『異端の空—太平洋戦争軍用機秘録』文春文庫。

WILLMOTT, H. P. 2005, *The Battle of Leyte Gulf: The Last Fleet Action.* Bloomington: Indiana University Press.

WILSON, George M. 1969, *Radical Nationalist in Japan: Kita Ikki, 1883—1937.* Harvard: Harvard University Press.

YAGAMI Kazuo 2006, *Konoe Fumimaro and the Failure of Peace in Japan, 1937-1941.* Jefferson, North Carolina, and London: McFarland & Company.

YAMAZAKI Masahiro 2017, *"Tennō kikan setsu" jiken.* Tōkyō: Shūeisha Shinsho.
山崎雅弘『「天皇機関説」事件』集英社新書。

YOKOTA Yutaka & HARRINGTON, Joseph D. 1962, *The Kaiten Weapon.* New York: Ballantine Books.

Yomiuri shinbun sengoshi hanhen (ed.) 1981, *Nisshōmaru jiken—Iran sekiyu wo motomete.* Tōkyō: Tōjusha.
読売新聞戦後史斑編『日章丸事件—イラン石油を求めて』冬樹社。

YOSHIDA Toshizumi 2003, *Mitogaku to Meiji ishin.* Tōkyō: Yoshikawa Kōbunkan.
吉田俊純『水戸学と明治維新』吉川弘文館。

YOSHIKAWA, Lisa 2017, *Making History Matter: Kuroita Katsumi and the Construction of Imperial Japan.* Cambridge (Mass.): Harvard University Asia Center.

Yūzankaku (ed.) 1938, *Nihongaku sōsho 4—Bukyō honron, Bukyō shōgaku, Bukyō zensho kōroku.* Tōkyō: Yūzankaku.
雄山閣編『日本學叢書 第4巻 武教本論・武教小学・武教全書講録』雄山閣。

———— (ed.) 1938, *Nihongaku sōsho 8—Seimeiron, Kyūmon ihan, Kōdōkan kijutsugi.* Tōkyō: Yūzankaku.
雄山閣編『日本學叢書 第8巻 正名論・及門遺範・弘道館記述義』雄山閣。

________ (ed.) 1938, *Nihongaku sōsho 2—Hōken taiki, Hōken taiki uchigi*. Tōkyō: Yūzankaku.
雄山閣編『日本學叢書 第 2 巻　保建大記・保建大記打聞』雄山閣。

www.ingramcontent.com/pod-product-compliance
Lightning Source LLC
LaVergne TN
LVHW051053180726
843512LV00019B/1459